T0078029

Other books by Dr. Robert Sneider PsyD

American Lynchpin; The Spirit of Freedom and the Second Civil War, Trafford
SSTOP: School Shooter Threat Onset Predictive,
The Pathology of Bullying, Violence in Schools and the School Shooter Syndrome
Strategic Book Publishing and Rights Company
www.sbpra.com

Novels by Robyrt Snyder

The Wycked Falls: Descent into the Maelstrom, Trafford
The Falls II: In the Crossfire of Mist and Madness, Trafford

AMERICAN CRUCIFIXION

THE PERSECUTION OF A CONSERVATIVE EDUCATOR AND THE BIRTH OF THE CANCEL CULTURE

Dr. Robert Sneider PsyD

Order this book online at www.trafford.com
or email orders@trafford.com

Most Trafford titles are also available at major online book retailers.

Disclaimer: This is a true story. Many of the names and places have been changed or omitted out of respect and for the protection of privacy of the individuals concerned. Naming individuals would have served no real purpose. It was the system that was rotten and needed to be exposed. This book is an indictment of that system.

Print information available on the last page.

ISBN: 978-1-6987-1213-0 (sc)
ISBN: 978-1-6987-1214-7 (e)

www.robyrtsnyder.com
www.trafford.com

Trafford rev. 06/23/2022

www.trafford.com

North America & international
toll-free: 844-688-6899 (USA & Canada)
fax: 812 355 4082

CONTENTS

Dedication vii
Introduction ix
Preface xiii

New World Beginnings: Initiation 1
Background 16
Learning The Ropes 33
Living in NYC 47
The Middle Years: The Good 62
The Tide Turns 75
The Persecution: The Bad 84
Trapped Like A Rat 110
The Big Picture 139
Epiphany 180

Afterword 195
Works Cited 199
Appendix A 201
Appendix B 203
Appendix C 205
Appendix D 213

DEDICATION

This book is dedicated to all the students who allowed me the honor and the privilege of teaching them, particularly the ones in the Bronx who are engaged in a daily struggle just to survive in the toughest of environments. I hope that I was able to—maybe even in just the smallest of ways—made your life better for having had me as your teacher. You taught me more about life than you will ever know and for that I am a better person.

This book is also dedicated to DB my friend and colleague and his spirit.

All he really wanted to do was just help kids in any way that he could and despite his flaws he should be recognized for that—something the cancel culture will never do. And for which he made the ultimate sacrifice.

And to God who always guides my thoughts and my hand whenever I write.

INTRODUCTION

Writing this book felt like taking the journey over again. It was an adventure when I lived it the first time and like many of life's adventures it was wrought with exhilaration and dark places—and everything in between. It certainly wasn't anything like I expected. Knowing what I know now I would never go back. I *could* never go back even if I wanted to because I wouldn't last five minutes in that environment at this stage of my life. I'm sure my heart would not be able to withstand it. But at the time I didn't have a single regret for the choice that I made to go there—even though everyone I knew told me that I was crazy. I was almost fifty years old at the time; I had a home in New Hampshire, and I had job security in the electronics field, after spending the last twenty-five years building up a career. I threw it all away to go live in a place I knew nothing about—to start a new career in a profession that I had virtually no experience. Yet I don't regret the decision. It certainly wasn't all roses. In fact, it might have been the most challenging thing I have ever done in my life. However, if nothing else, there was never a dull moment. For a good portion of it I was scared out of my wits.

And yet I wouldn't have missed a minute of it for the world.

It was an experience that would splash paint on everything that I would do afterwards.

Sometimes the dark stuff is what I remember the most. I've always maintained that I loved the profession, but I hated the system and because of my experience with the system; it has spawned a deep-rooted cynicism that I'm not sure I wanted to revisit by writing this book. They say that time has a tendency of erasing the bad memories and leaving only the good ones. That hasn't happened yet. Maybe I have not been away from it long enough. Maybe the current political climate in this country has continued to remind me of what I had to endure. Maybe it's just too engrained.

I remember one summer vacation while I was still teaching in the Bronx, I found myself watching the series The Wire. For those of you who aren't familiar with it, part of it is about teaching school in the inner city of Philadelphia, I believe. I couldn't get through it. It was so reminiscent of the situation I found myself in in the Bronx, that even though I didn't have to go back to school for a few months just the thought of it would send chills down my spine. I would break out in a cold sweat, and I couldn't sleep at night, whenever I watched an episode that particularly struck home. That is the effect that just watching a *fictional* characterization would do to me.

The transitions into that world were some of the worst times of my life. It was like going into a foreign country—one that was in a permanent state of war with the world outside and I was the main target in the shooting gallery. Every other week I would go to my home in New Hampshire for the weekend. When I told my family and friends that I was going to New York City to pursue a career in teaching, they all advised me that I should sell my property in New Hampshire. For some reason I did not and after experiencing the chaos that my life soon became in New York, I was never so grateful that I had not followed through on their advice. My home in New Hampshire was on a two-acre wooded lot in a sleepy, little country town, 20 minutes from the coast. I never fully appreciated its serenity and peacefulness until I lived in the zoo that was New York City. Coming home every two weeks to the quiet, the fresh air and the smell of woodsmoke was what kept me sane for all those years in the Bronx. The smell of woodsmoke was then—and always will be until the day I die—an embrace that I was back home in the arms of New Hampshire. That and a mournful, ghostly train whistle somewhere far off in the distant night.

Many times, especially after a week or two of vacation the dread of going back into the maelstrom and stress of my job was simply overwhelming. Often the night before going back into the classroom was sleepless and wrought with tears. I'm not ashamed to admit it. I don't regard myself as a person that cries easily, but I was reduced to tears on more than one occasion. However, as you read on you will see that I was caught in a trap. In order to survive, I had to gird myself with a whole different persona, one that was steeled to withstand the rigors of the environment to which I was once again returning. I had to summon that strength from somewhere and so I prayed.

"Dear Lord, give me the strength to do what I have to do to get through this day."

It was an open-ended prayer because I never knew what challenges I was going to face and all I wanted was to do my job and get through one day at a time. I would worry about tomorrow when it came and in my present mindset that was a million miles away.

Any illusion that I had that I was going to change the world was dispelled early on. I just wanted to help these kids the best way that I could. That was the way I lived every day of my life for the fifteen years I spent in the system.

The left has long used the education system as the microcosm for society. It was the original template.

The guerrilla tactics employed by democrats to take down President Donald Trump, eventually evolved into a blatant, frontal assault on our freedoms and our democracy, through the nullification of 63 million Americans who voted for this President in 2016. Those tactics are known today as the cancel culture. The genesis of those same tactics was rooted in the education system.

Before the war was declared on President Trump, conservative educators were in the trenches fighting against destructive liberal policies in a battle for the minds of our children. They were fighting for American principles, they were fighting for their rights, they were fighting for their jobs, and they were fighting for their lives.

After WWII and during the time that I attended school the ratio of conservative teachers to liberal teachers in the public school system was on the order 2 to 3. When I was teaching that ratio was in the range of 15 or 20 to 1. Today it is probably 50 to 1.

I was not a born teacher. I was 50 years old before I stepped in front of my first class of students. I had no illusions that I was going to change the world. But I did think that I could help kids to learn. That's all I ever wanted to do. What I discovered was that I had a talent for just that—helping kids learn. I had found my niche.

In the next 6 years I would achieve certifications in 5 subjects and teaching licenses in 3 states. I would complete an Associates, a Bachelors, 2 Masters and a Doctorate degree. I was a mentor for two of NYC's most prestigious initiatives. I founded and edited the first newspaper in my school's history. I was responsible for the first ever visit to my school of the Museum of Natural History's mobile learning center. I successfully taught in one of the harshest environments in the country—the Bronx, NY. I was at the apex of my career.

Fast forward just a few years and I could not even get a job as a teacher's assistant. How was it possible to fall so far so fast? I ran into the face of evil—cancel culture. My only crime—I was a conservative.

This is the story of a conservative educator trying to survive in a corrupted liberal education system.

PREFACE

Just so you know right from the start, I am going to come right out and say it, I AM A RACIST. Through and through. No doubt about it. And not just any kind of racist, not just your ordinary run of the mill racist. Oh no, I am the worst kind of racist according to the left. And if they say it then it MUST be true because this is a tactic that they have been cultivating for many years particularly in the education system, but more on that later.

The left says I am a racist because of the evidence. First of all, I am a conservative =racist. I committed the ultimate sin; I voted for Donald Trump= ultimate racist. In fact, I voted for him twice= double ultimate racist. If that alone is not enough to convict, there is far more evidence for consideration.

I never got vaccinated for Covid=racist. I believe in law and order and that our laws should be enforced=racist. I believe that our police should be funded and supported=racist. I believe that all demonstrations of violence should be condemned including the demonstration on the Capital on January 6th, 2020, but also all the riots the previous summer conducted by Black Lives Matter and Antifa=racist. I believe our borders should be secure from illegal immigration=racist, and our elections should be fair and secure and require identification to vote=racist.

I also believe that our schools should not be indoctrinating our children with gender and critical race theories=racist. I am against teacher unions=racist and I believe that parents should have school choice=racist. I believe that parents have the right to express their opinions to the school board concerning their child's education without being labelled "domestic terrorists" by the FBI= racist. I believe that students should be taught to read and write and most importantly to think critically for themselves=most definitely racist and an enemy of the state.

I believe in the Constitution=racist, the First Amendment=racist and the Second Amendment=racist. I believe in freedom, our country and I salute our flag= racist, racist, racist.

50 years ago, these beliefs would have been considered mainstream.
40 years ago, this credo would have been regarded as the right to express your own opinion.
30 years ago, this credo would have been labelled contrarian.
20 years ago, I would have been worthy of cancellation.
10 years ago, anyone like this was a racist.

"woke" – alert to injustice in society, especially racism.

"Cancel culture" – is a blanket term used to refer to a modern form of ostracism in which someone is thrust out of social or professional circles—whether it be online, on social media, or in person. Those subject to this ostracism are said to have been "cancelled".

Today in 2022 someone espousing these beliefs is a deplorable, white supremacist (even if you are not white) domestic terrorist, racist, deserving of doxing, censoring, cancellation, destruction and even death. Even crucifixion as indicated in the title. What progress we have made as a country and a society. We should be proud of ourselves. We know at least half the country is because they even refer to themselves as progressives. According to these progressives the country is on the right path even if it means denouncing and disenfranchising one half of the country's fellow citizens and denying them their rights in a democratic republic founded on freedom, individual liberty, and the Constitution. Progressives are perfectly fine with that.

Today the Department of Justice has determined that any parent who goes to a school board meeting and voices their opinion against what is being taught in their child's school such as critical race theory, sexism or transgenderism is a "domestic terrorist" and is subject to arrest and prosecution.

Today the Department of Homeland Security has determined that anyone that verbally objects to any Covid 19 protocol or raises a concern that the 2020 election was compromised is designated as a "violent, domestic terrorist" to be listed as such by other law enforcement entities such as the FBI and the CIA and can be surveilled, censored, and prosecuted at their discretion.

Today if you question any part of the leftist agenda, you are labelled a systemic racist, a white supremacist, a sexist, a misogynist, a fascist, a neo-Nazi or a terrorist. Take your pick.

These used to be basic rights protected by the Constitution. The right to free speech, the right to assemble, the right to protest peacefully, the right to due process. Now if you are on the wrong side of an issue (wrong side being defined as anything in disagreement with the left) because you are a conservative your rights can be suspended, and the Constitution doesn't apply. In today's vernacular you can be cancelled. This is progress in the eyes of leftists. What it really is, is tyranny coming soon to a town near you.

Apparently today everything that I say, think and do is racist and the left tells it to my face every day. They make sure that I know that I am a despicable human being and the worst kind of racist that every walked on the face of the earth and worthy of cancellation and destruction. After all the evidence is irrefutable. In their eyes their case has been made.

I wonder if there was anything that would or could change their opinion of me? I wonder if they would change their mind if they knew that despite holding all the same beliefs that I do now I did something of extraordinary significance to aid one of their purported causes—something very few people would ever consider doing or would ever do?

Twenty years ago, as a white teacher from New Hampshire (one of the most homogenous states in the union) I went into the dark bowels of the inner city in the Bronx, New York with the intention of educating poverty-stricken minorities. I worked with Title One, special needs students who are the most difficult to teach and the most difficult population to recruit teachers to serve. I wonder if it would make any difference to them that the population of the school that I was assigned to was 99% black and Hispanic? Out of 1600 students and around 200 school personnel, only a handful of people were white. The community around the school also reflected those percentages and not only did I just teach in that community for almost a decade, but I lived amongst the people of that community.

It was a complete reversal from where I had come from. It often felt like I was the only white guy around. And yet even though my service to that community doesn't fit the narrative of the left, I would still be a racist in their determination because I wasn't right in the mind. To them and their twisted logic it would make perfect sense for someone like me (the worst kind of racist) to go to such a place where he would be inundated by black and Hispanic people. Where he would be a minority for the first time in his life. Isn't that the kind of place where all white people aspire to go, never mind those who are racist? But that is the logic or lack thereof of the left and there is no reasoning with it, especially once you have been labeled. It's the same kind of logic that labels black people as white supremacists and Jewish people as Nazis. It makes no sense, and it knows no bounds. And that is what sets it apart from anything that had come before it. It is the logic of the cancel culture (it wasn't called by this name back then) and we conservatives in the education system were the first to witness its birth and experience its persecutions.

Earlier I mentioned that the left of today is willing to go to great lengths to achieve their goals even the destruction of their opponents. I don't use the terms death and destruction lightly, although I'm sure some of you reading this now are thinking these are exaggerations or figures of speech. When I first went into this field, I would have agreed with you, but I can assure you they are not exaggerations. Unfortunately, it was the case back then and this book will bear that out and it is the case today.

Much of what we have learned about the left has been brought out by the election of Donald Trump in 2016. If we have learned anything about the left it is that their goals and their only goals are power and control. Secondly, they will do anything including the death and destruction of anything that comes between them and the attainment of those goals. It is only since Trump that conservatives have begun to realize that we are in a war and that we have to start fighting back. Most liberals do not believe in God. One of the consequences of this doctrine is that God has been successfully removed from our public schools. Politics is their god and politics for them has no morals. Today it has never been clearer that we are in a battle for not only the soul of our country but for our own existential souls. It is a war between good and evil. Although I didn't know it at the time this book is the story of my personal battle against that insidious face of evil. For me it was a journey into the belly of the beast.

If you ever find yourself driving south on Route 95 towards Manhattan, the George Washington Bridge, and the New Jersey border, most of the territory you are in before you get to any of those destinations, is the Bronx. It's a big sprawling place, one of the five boroughs of New York City. It is the home of Yankee Stadium, The Bronx Zoo, and the Botanical Gardens. Those are well known travel destinations. Those areas were not where my school was located. As you travel down 95 the buildings, the overpasses and the bridges for whatever reason become darker, blacker, scarier and the graffiti becomes thicker. When you are in this area, you are glad as a traveler that you are just passing through and that you do not have to take one of these exits. That is the exit ramp where I got off and would spend the next chunk of my life living and teaching.

Teaching and just trying to survive.

NEW WORLD BEGINNINGS: INITIATION

It was an unusually steamy morning in late August 2004 when I found myself, staring out into the schoolyard from the third-floor window of a junior high school in the Bronx, New York. The students had assembled for the first day of the school year and were preparing to make their way up to the classrooms. Other than a stint as a practice teacher when I was 19 years old, I had never spent a single minute as an educator. I had spent the last 20 years as an electronic technician in the high-tech industry.

That summer I had quit my job (a job, by the way, which had paid very well and provided job security) against the advice of my friends and co-workers and to the horror of my family and relatives and signed up for the 'New York City Urban Teachers' program. This was a program that would assist me in getting all the necessary teaching licenses and certifications and subsidize a master's degree in special education, in return for teaching two years of special education in an inner-city, Title I school. I also had to accept a 50% cut in pay, and relocation to one of the most crowded cities on the planet.

I was in the midst of a career change, and this was a fellowship program similar to 'Teach for America', that brought teachers from all over the country to high need areas of education, such as special education, in troubled schools and depressed and poverty-stricken environments. The philosophy of the program was to try to bring teachers from the outside of the neighborhoods where these schools were located, in order to break the cycle of poor-quality education, perpetrated by poorly educated students, who would then become future teachers and continue the process by passing on their deficient skills to the next generation of students. It goes without saying that these were difficult jobs under difficult circumstances.

The average teacher who has established themselves with a good job in a good school is not the one willing to trade that, to work in a much harsher environment. So, these programs, such as 'Teach for America' and other Fellows programs, were designed to offer incentives for educators to go into these deficient and dysfunctional settings and try to improve the quality of education. That's how a middle-aged, Caucasian man, embarking on a new career, found himself smack in the middle of the Bronx, New York, about to receive his first class ever.

It was a huge risk, to be sure, but it was not my lack of experience that was worrying me at this juncture. As I scanned the schoolyard from my third-floor vantage point, I began to realize that there was something that I had not been prepared for and that no one had bothered to mention up to this point. Either they assumed that I knew what I was getting into, or they didn't want me to quit before I started. The composition of the students in the schoolyard was 99% African American and Hispanic. My trepidation was not so much about the skin color of the students but what it represented—a different culture. I knew nothing about the African American culture, about the Hispanic culture and about the general culture of the inner-city environment. That's when it dawned on me how much of a fish-out-of-water I was.

I was born and had grown up in Canada. I don't know if it was the cold and the snow but there just weren't many black persons in Canada, in those days. The first time I even saw a black person in the flesh was when I crossed over the border into Niagara Falls, New York with my friends, when I was fifteen years old, to do some underage drinking. A few years later, I went to college in an upscale enclave of Massachusetts where essentially the only persons of color on that campus were on scholarship to the basketball team. Years later, I would buy a home in New Hampshire which is arguably one of the whitest states in the union. One time a teacher who had grown up in the diverse environment of New York City visited me and was astounded at how homogenous the population was. It was the truth. I remember being at Hampton Beach on a sweltering Fourth of July with a hundred thousand beachgoers and you would have a hard time finding a person of color. The point I am trying to illustrate, is that when it came to the subject of diversity, I had led a very sheltered life

Now not only was I being exposed to diversity in the extreme (for the first time in my life I was a minority in the most dramatic sense), but I was expected to teach these students. Teach them…I had no understanding of what they were about. I had always been under the impression that in order to teach something, you had to have an understanding of your subject and your audience. I certainly had no understanding of my audience.

Whatever confidence I had that I could handle the situation, was quickly eroding. My concern was turning to abject fear. I felt the walls closing in on me while the floor (and my life) was collapsing under my feet. I have to confess that I had thoughts of running for the nearest exit—that this was all a big mistake and that I needed to go back to my nice safe life.

"Who needs THIS" I asked myself.
"Not me" I answered myself.

You know you're in real trouble when you find yourself engaged in a two-way conversation, but you are the only one in the room. I was at one of those crucial crossroads in life where the next decision you make will likely determine how the rest of your life goes. Looking back, this was certainly borne out. Then I thought, why was I doing this in the first place? I was doing it because I felt I was at a time in my life when I needed to give something back to others. I had done the private sector thing in pursuit of a paycheck and all its materialism and found it to be lacking. There was something missing in my life. I was restless. I was searching for more purpose. So maybe in the end I did need this.

And maybe—just maybe— they needed what I had to offer. I would never know if I walked out now and the only way, I was going to find out is if I stuck around, so I guess in the end it was my curiosity that got the best of me. And culture shock, be damned. Besides, if you view life as a journey then this was just another adventure along the path, and sometimes it's not always about what you learn about the world around you, but what you learn about yourself. After all, one of the tenets of my upbringing was that strength and character was bred from conquering adversity. Adversity was the necessary fire that tempered the steel.

What happened next became the template for the rest of the time that I would spend in the Bronx. I became the student. The students would teach me. They would teach me their culture. I had heard that old teacher's saw that "The kids teach me as much as I teach them" and I never really understood what that meant. In the end, they taught me enough to enable me to write this book. Without them, this book would not have been possible and to them this book is dedicated.

The bell rang and the students were on their way up to the classrooms. Having made the decision to stay and see it through, I didn't have much time.

I tried to focus on the task at hand. My immediate concern was how should I greet the students? Should I stand in my doorway as they entered, or should I be seated at my desk? We had been taught in our training that standing at the doorway presented a more authoritarian presence, in which you controlled the situation right from the get-go. However, I opted for the more casual presentation of being seated at my desk, as I hoped that this would be more informal and put the students more at ease. This also had the advantage of hiding my knees, which were knocking pretty badly at this point in the proceedings.

I was soon in for a rude awakening. The first student through my door was a huge kid, at least 6 foot tall and African American and I thought to myself,

this is an eighth grader...it's a good thing I didn't sign up for high school... what are they feeding these kids nowadays, anyway?

He walked right over to the front of my desk and placed his hands on my desk, looked me straight in the eye and proclaimed

"I hate school, I hate teachers and I'm not going to do a F... ing thing you tell me to do."

I had already programmed myself into asking the obligatory,

"How was your summer vacation?"

which I blurted out right on cue, just as I had rehearsed it and in juxtaposition to what he had just declared, this seemed awkwardly incongruent. This only evoked a look of condescension and he spat out

"It sucked and what's it to you anyway?"

as he made his way to his seat. First rule a teacher should learn—listen to what your students are telling you. And so, it began. My initiation.

So much for putting them at ease.

It was in this manner that my teaching career was launched, and I had walked through the door into a whole new world. I will make this comment on my initiation—this would later be verified as we progressed through the school year—that this student, who I will call student A was true to his word and even made good on things he had not enunciated. He despised school and teachers and operated pretty much on his own schedule, with little fear of school-dispensed repercussions. However, I came to appreciate student A and his direct style, whether you liked him or not, because at least he was upfront with you. There were others who were much more insidious with their intentions but right now, I had more pressing problems to deal with.

By the way, in case I haven't mentioned it, I had been hired to teach science—a subject for which I had no license or certification. The New York Department of Education, in their infinite wisdom, designated me as a science teacher. It was at this point that I began to wonder about the judgement of my employers. It was a content area in which I had not taken a course since high school some 30 years ago— but apparently it was a situation in which the New York City Department of Education, in its infinite wisdom, deemed me eminently qualified.

Despite a lack of certification to teach science, I was told not to worry, because it would be covered under the umbrella of my special education license. I did have a special education certification and it was under that canopy that I was allowed to teach virtually any subject. In theory anyway.

I guess that covered the legality of the situation, but I was worried about something else, that I considered of far more importance.

I didn't have any knowledge of science.

The last time I had even been in a science class was in high school.

I had no training as a science teacher and for that matter, no teacher training whatsoever from the New York City Department of Education (NYCDOE). That didn't seem to bother anybody, except me. Leave it up to the NYCDOE to not let a little detail like that get in the way. I was told that the science opening was where they had the need and that was the position available and if I wanted to teach, I would have to take it or leave it.

I did want to teach so I took it.

But if I didn't know better (and here I will use a term from my previous tenure in the private sector) I was beginning to get the suspicion that I was being "set up to fail."

That was just the beginning of my problems or to tap into my extensive scientific knowledge and phrase it in more technical terms— it was just the tip of the iceberg. Boy were these kids in for a real treat. They were getting a teacher that didn't know much more about the subject than they did. Maybe even less. That was a secret that they were probably better off not knowing and I certainly wasn't going to tell them. The only question was whether I could keep them from finding out on their own how much a magic show this was going to be. I didn't know if I was that good of a magician. From there the situation only got worse.

Least of which was that I had no textbooks or course materials. Another situation in which the NYCDOE didn't seem overly concerned about. In fact, there was not a stitch of instructive material in the entire classroom including the walls and shelves of this third-floor hothouse. There I was on the third floor of a brick building that had no air conditioning save for an ancient electric fan in the corner that looked like it was a refugee from the forties. I soon learned that the way to calculate the temperature in your room was to take the outside temperature and add 10° for each floor that you went up. So, for instance if it was 80° outside, the second floor would be 90* and the third floor would be 100°— especially in afternoons when the sun came through our windows and baked us like worms under a magnifying glass.

I was quickly beginning to see why so many teachers washed out in the first few years of this profession. It's no wonder that in this kind of brutal environment 50% of teachers quit during their first year in teaching, 75% are gone by second year and by the fifth year only 10% of teachers remain in the profession. It seemed that the approach of the school and the DOE was to provide new teachers with the worst possible conditions and see who survived. It was almost a designed trial by fire.

I personally don't agree with this approach, whether by design or accident and I think the system would be better served by providing more support to new teachers but strange as it may seem, this strategy actually worked with me, and it made me a better teacher. At the time, though, I was doing anything I could just to survive. It was a throwback to my days in the subdivision where survival of the fittest was the rule of the day and you had to confront your adversity. If it had not been for the training of that early experience in my life, I can guarantee I would not have lasted in this environment. The janitors in the building had a betting pool against how long I would last, and the long end bet had me out by the end of the week. Even I had to concede the overly optimistic folly of that wager.

There's an old adage that sailors recite when they are caught in a storm and the ship is in extreme peril, that I found applied to this situation perfectly. They talk about when 'the waves turn the minutes to hours.' That had to be the longest week of my life. Every time I looked at the clock it seemed to be running backward. Imagine yourself in front of 35 minority kids whose culture you didn't understand, who had no use for education and didn't want to be there, in a room that was 100 degrees, with no educational materials of any kind. I did everything I could think of—told stories, asked questions, led the class in physical exercises, brought in newspapers for current events. One day we found an ancient computer, in pieces, in one of the closets.

This might have been the first computer that Adam and Eve ever used but I didn't care. My previous background was in high-tech, and I knew a little bit about hardware and software and so the class project became to put this computer back together. At that point I didn't care if it worked or not—just trying to put it back together would be enough to keep the class occupied, at least for a while and after all this was science class. The bonus, to the astonishment of all of us, was that once we had it assembled, it not only worked but the printer printed. And aside from computers in the administrative offices, we had the only other working computer in the entire school.

I never knew at the time what a boon this would prove to be for my situation. There was nothing that these kids, poor as they were, related to more than technology. When you came right down to it, they were actually quite computer savvy and so not only could we use the computer for researching and learning about content, but it was a great incentive for them to be granted the privilege to go on it, when they had completed their regular lessons. It was nothing less than a Godsend and it literally saved my teaching career. I learned early on how technology could be incorporated into the classroom and if used properly, what a tool it could be to enhance student engagement and academic performance. That was a lifesaver, and I had my technical expertise in my previous life to thank for it. What better example of cooperative learning? We were all in this together. That's how I survived my first week.

My takeaway from my first week was I vowed that never again would I be caught without alternatives. Teaching in this environment required that if something is not working you need to be ready to pivot to something else no matter how much preparation you put into plan A. Because of the volatility of this student population, you needed to have a plan B and C. There was a saying that some of the veterans passed on to us rookies and it was one that rang true.

If you don't have a plan for your students, they will have a plan for you."

Translation: If you don't keep them engaged, they will be open for mayhem.

To me that meant that I needed alternatives in my classroom that I could turn to at a moments' notice even if it meant shelving the planned lesson for that day. It was like waving a shiny object in front of the students.

Hey, you didn't like what I was doing before, now look at this.

I know what you are saying, "That's not really teaching."

And you would be correct. But it was better than having the class deteriorate into physical violence. Teachers who were so wedded to their lesson plans were usually the ones that had the worst classroom behaviors and ultimately the lowest performing classes academically. At least that was my observation with teachers in this environment. Consequently, I stocked my room with every visual I could lay my hands on, books, hands on materials, smartboards computers, animals (more on that later). I would spend my own money, if necessary, but I looked at it as the cost of doing business. All told I spent thousands of dollars of my salary on ensuring that I was providing a learning ecosystem with plenty of alternatives.

Once you enter this world there is a period of adjustment that is required. If you are not familiar with this environment, you are going to have to get acclimated because there are going to be some things that you have probably never encountered.

The first thing I noticed that was different from the private sector was that everything in the field of education is couched in an acronym. Every industry employs acronyms to a certain extent, but I have never been in a field of employment that uses so many acronyms, that it is like they are all talking in a foreign language. If you find sections of this story are laden with acronyms, that was done on purpose to give you, the reader a sense of how prevalent (and in my opinion how ridiculous) this practice is.

I think it is a veteran of the system's way of either intimidating or impressing a newcomer with their insider knowledge. It signals to the neophyte that "Hey I'm no tenderfoot, I'm a member of the club." If only they thought, it was as important to express their knowledge of their subject matter. But then that would only expose how unknowledgeable they really are.

"Better to remain silent and be thought a fool than to speak and remove all doubt." (Attributed to Abraham Lincoln)

The next thing that struck me was the noise level in the building. It can be deafening at times. For some reason these kids are very vocal. They are always talking, singing, yelling, rapping. It is all you can do to get them to be quiet so that classroom learning can be conducted. It was the number one struggle of any teacher in this building. I have been in classrooms since New York and every one was much quieter. I was in a high school in New Hampshire that issued every student their own laptop computer. Everything was done on that computer to the point that I saw a teacher who was sitting right next to a student communicate only by their computers. There was no verbal or personal interaction. In my estimation this is going a little too far in the direction of an impersonal nature, but it explains why the classrooms in this school were so quiet.

The third thing that strikes you when you can discern *what* they are saying is the level of profanity. They are always cursing, using derogatory rap lyrics, name calling. Few people were singled out and disciplined for it. It is so pervasive in this culture that it had become an accepted form of discourse. I was not used to this on a regular basis. Sure, I've been in situations where there was a certain amount of "locker room" talk but this was on another level. I have to say that there were many days where I would come home and feel like I had been in a pornographic movie all day. My ears were burning from all the graphic language they had been exposed to.

This led to the fourth revelation in my initiation. Everything with these kids is sexualized and there is a real lack of boundaries. They see you as being one of them. These are 12, 13-year-old kids and even 10- and 11-year-olds and they are obsessed with sex. It dominates their lives. It's what they watch on television and on the internet, it's what they think about, it's what they talk about, it's what they do. Many of the girls drop out before they finish eighth grade because they wind up pregnant and have to raise their child. They will have sex in a dim corner of a school hallway if they think they can get away with it.

As a rookie teacher I used to have to park on the street until I got enough seniority to rate one of the parking spots on school property. I was assigned a spot in a courtyard area behind the school. When I was teaching in the after-school program and I was ready to leave at 7 o'clock at night, I would purposely make a lot of noise before I went out the rear exit door so that I would not have to walk into any sexual activity that was taking place out there. I've had female students sitting in the back of the classroom flashing their breasts. I had a 12-year-old girl ride her bike up to me on the school playground and ask me out on a date. I was 50 years old at the time. What was she going to do, pick me up on her bike? I could not believe that I constantly had to remind these students that I was their teacher, and I was not one of them.

Finally, a newcomer into this territory will be struck by the constant physicality. Everyone has their hands on someone else. I wish I had a penny for every time I told a student to keep their hands to themselves. There were lots of fights and other altercations and most occurred inside the classroom. There was a strange ritualistic dance that I had never seen before that was common practice before any altercation ensued. The two combatants usually the boys but I saw it with girls too would square off and then come together and bump chests. It was like two goats ramming each other. This might occur several times before punches started flying. Many teachers and paraprofessionals spent a good chunk of their time breaking up fights. It was one of the main reasons that school personnel were always getting hurt or terminated for inappropriate conduct. There will be much more on this subject in the upcoming pages of this book.

In the course of MY education. I witnessed and learned many things about the culture of this new world that I had entered. And many of these things had more to do with the culture of poverty in the inner-city. There were two incidents in particular that illustrated what a neophyte I was, when it came to the culture that I was now immersed. As I had stated, my class was composed of minorities—African Americans and Hispanics but all were of a dark skin color so that to my untrained and naïve eye it was difficult to distinguish one group from the other. As I was calling on students who had raised their hands, one student asked me why I was such a racist. I was taken aback. I had always thought that the term racist applied to a white and black situation. There were no white kids that I was favoring over any of the black kids because there were no white kids, period. I asked him to explain. "You keep calling on the Hispanics over us African Americans." I was blown away.

Because I had limited exposure to minorities, I was not able to distinguish such subtle differences but obviously there were vast differences to those concerned. I was being schooled in one of the more unattractive traits of human nature. I soon began to realize the culture in these inner-city schools is one of divisiveness. No matter how similar people appear to be, they will strive to find the differences that set them apart. Because once they have defined the differences, they can exploit those to put down other people in order to build themselves up. This is a practice that has been going on since the beginning of time. I remember one student being teased ruthlessly because his parents had bought him the wrong brand of sneakers.

I can honestly say that in my time as a teacher in this environment skin color was never an issue. You quickly become color blind and your only concern becomes who exhibits good behavior and who exhibits bad behavior. I can say that even in this environment there were students who had been instilled with values and morals that I would have hoped to have fostered in my own kids and that was a real credit to the parents who had raised them. In this place, it was like trying to grow a rose between the cracks of a sidewalk.

Another time, I was teaching a class of 8th graders who just happened to consist of all boys. After the lesson, we were having some cooperative time when one of the students asked for permission to play a radio. It was granted. During these times, there is usually a high level of discussion. I was doing some work at my desk when I noticed that it was unusually silent, except for a song that was lightly playing in the background. This was a group of especially tough kids—kids who wouldn't cry if they were cut with a knife and I noticed that many were sobbing to themselves. I asked the student sitting closest to me what was going on. He said that there was a rap song playing with the theme of "I never knew my father" or something to that extent.

I still didn't get it, "So?"

"So", he explained, "None of us knew our fathers".

You could have knocked me over with a feather. I had no concept of how pervasive the deterioration of the family was in the inner city, until that moment. Twenty kids and not one had a relationship with their natural father. Amazing. It was then that I realized I had no idea of what these kids went through or what their life was like when they left school.

There were other "rules" that I was introduced to. Many teachers were advocates of the "broken window" philosophy. In layman's terms it meant that if a teacher was strict with the little indiscretions in the classroom it would head off the larger infractions. There was some merit to this theory, but I found out that this might not apply to my population of special education students. One area that other teachers were able to implement this practice was in conjunction with their bathroom policy. Some teachers prohibited any student from going to the bathroom during their class. Students were required to "hold it" until the end of the class.

My students were on all kinds of medications from Ritalin to anti-depressives to anti-aggression medicines. These had all kinds of side effects from sleepiness to nausea to thirst and frequent trips to the bathroom. I almost learned the hard way that imposing bathroom restrictions was going to be detrimental. One day I was sitting at my desk attired in one of my best suits. This was before I realized that it was better to dress casual because you were more than likely going to spend a good part of your day on the floor wrestling with some unruly students or trying to break up a fight.

A student approached me and was about to ask for permission to go to the bathroom. I noticed that he appeared to be a little green around the gills. Something told me to get up and get out of my seat. Just as I did, not barely a second later he opened his mouth and blew a stream of vomit all across my desk and over the chair that I had just vacated. I would have been covered from head to toe.

I realized that bathroom privilege was an area that could be abused but I never ever denied a student his request to go to the bathroom. Most of these kids had legitimate reasons and even if I was taken advantage of a few times, I would rather give them the benefit of the doubt than have a lot of "accidents" in my class. I think they appreciated it as well because it saved everybody a lot of embarrassment. Sure, it was important to have discipline, but this was just not a hill that I was willing to die on.

For some students staying awake during class was always a challenge because of some of their medications. At least I like to think it was that and not because my lesson was boring. Sometimes I would play a game where I had a dollar bill attached to a string and I would drag it over them if I noticed their head was down on their desk. If they felt it and woke up in time to grab it, they got to keep it. Not exactly orthodox but it did get their attention.

Giving out rewards in the form of candy was always another controversial issue. Many teachers frowned on it as an incentive and others believed it was tantamount to committing suicide by supplying sugar to already hyperactive students. I always felt in some of the impoverished schools that it was almost a source of nutrition as long as it was done in moderation. I always checked beforehand with the parents to see if they permitted it for their child. How much things have changed? Nowadays schools administer contraceptives and sex change drugs without the parents' consent or even their knowledge in some cases.

In many ways this was a bleak teaching environment, and the desperation was palpable. It was a world of concrete and cold steel where gangs ruled the streets at night. Just down the road from the school was a city park where a murder had been committed during my tenure.

Urban parks in this part of the Bronx are such pathetic excuses for trying to provide some nature and greenery amidst the onslaught of steel and concrete. They reek of sparseness and desperate lives. Anything that can be stolen is gone. Basketball courts never have nets and rarely have hoops. Flat surfaces are covered in graffiti three times over. This particular park had a murky body of water with a sewer pipe emptying into it. There were few trees, the grass was threadbare and there was garbage and litter everywhere.

I once took a class on a tour thinking I could educate them on some of the elements of nature. In my naiveté, I must have been confusing it with a trip through a park in New Hampshire where one was likely to find all kinds of wildlife to point out. We did see some birds and squirrels, but we saw a lot more needles and used condoms. One of these condoms was hanging from a bush and a student actually had the temerity to ask me what kind of bush it was. I responded with the only thing that came to mind.

"If I'm not mistaken that's a rubber tree."

(There was a teacher on that trip with me and every time he tells that story he breaks down with laughter.)

At one point in our sad attempt at a "nature trip" we came upon a small field. We hadn't got three steps into it when a man and a woman's heads popped up from the weeds. They were both naked in the middle of a sex act. That was enough nature for one day.

BACKGROUND

How did someone like me get to be somewhere like here?

My experience with and in schools was a lot different than anything that I was about to encounter in the Bronx. I was educated in the Canadian school system primarily in the 1960s. It was a different time and a different place. It was not politically correct, to say the least and in fact some of the things I am about to describe might horrify today's parents.

In all the years I spent inside the schools there I can never remember a fight taking place inside a classroom and I attribute that largely to the way discipline was meted out. And rarely did a fight occur on school grounds although in the heat of the activities during recess, sometimes it was inevitable. But a fight on school property had huge repercussions beyond what was incurred in the actual fight itself. It would involve teachers and the principal, detentions, and possibly corporal punishment. Yes, you heard that correctly. Corporal punishment was acceptable in those days, and it seemed teachers were always laying their hands on us in some form or another whether unarmed, or with an object intended to enhance the experience.

The preferred method of punishment at my grade school was The Strap. It was a two foot long by two-inch-wide strip of leather about double the thickness of an average belt. It was usually applied to the hands, but I had heard of some getting struck on the backside. The number of strokes depended on the crime committed. The intensity could depend on many factors. Such things like whether it was your first or tenth offense. Or how big the principle was—a big, tall man had much more leverage than a shorter man however I had one principal who compensated for his short stature by jumping into the air as he delivered the downstroke, and this contributed considerably to the force of the blow. I've seen golfers use the same principle to drive a golf ball further.

The final factor was how much the executioner liked you or hated you. I remember a fourth-grade teacher who either hated his job or just hated kids or both. There are always good and bad people in their profession however there are some people who should just not be teachers. This man was one of those. His hair was cut in a square crewcut and everything I remember about the man was that he was square and rigid. Cold and cruel with no sense of empathy. I've always believed to be a good teacher that you had to come from a place that you liked kids and that you genuinely cared about your students. I've always felt that had to be your default position because that is what would carry you through the ups and downs of the job and believe me there would be plenty of those. And a little enthusiasm for your job or the subject that you were teaching— I found through personal experience—could be contagious. You could still be tough and strict in the classroom if the kids sensed that you cared about them but if they sensed that they really didn't mean anything to you then you were just a disciplinarian and nothing else. As a student you would comply because of fear and nothing else. I don't believe that real learning takes place because of fear of your teacher.

Generally, when the punishment by The Strap was warranted, it was referred to the principal, but this particular gentleman preferred to administer The Strap to his students personally. I think it was the sadist in him. In fact, he seemed to relish the inflicting of pain that it caused. For all we knew we had a genuine dyed-in-the-wool sadist in our midst because this man always had a scowl on his face. The only time we ever saw him with a smile was after doling out a strapping.

Getting The Strap was much like being whipped across the hands except the strap—being wider than a whip—it usually didn't cut the flesh. However, the sound was like the crack of a whip and the pain of the blow was a shock that went right to your brain. Initially your hands went numb after the first blow but then your hands would turn red and swell up like balloons. The stinging and swelling would often last the rest of the day and was akin to wearing a pair of gloves on your hands.

The Strap, at the very least brought tears to your eyes. That was an unavoidable consequence for even the toughest kids. It was okay to cry out when being struck and cry afterwards and most kids did. Anyone who had been strapped understood. You were often allowed to sit in an outer office to compose yourself before you went back to class and that was the real measure. You did not want to go back to class and *still* be crying. That was unacceptable if you wanted to save face.

This particular sadist teacher got a dose of his own medicine one time. He used to wind up and put every ounce of his weight behind the descending blow to inflict the maximum amount of pain and illicit the most satisfaction. One time as he was really leaning into his down stroke a kid had the suicidal bravery (or maybe it was just a primal reflex action) to move his hand out of the way of The Strap. The Strap continued its descent until it struck the next object in its path which happened to be groin area of the teacher. This particular student said that he thought he saw actual flames come out of the eyes and ears of the teacher before he crumpled to the floor in agony. The kid informed the secretary, who in turn summoned the principal and the school nurse and it must have been quite embarrassing for the teacher to have them all gathered around him as the kid was sent back to class. I imagine that after this incident there was something, other than a pair of hands, that were swelled up like red balloons. We never saw our teacher for the rest of the day. Some people just shouldn't be teachers.

However strange as it may seem to kids today, corporal punishment was preferable—to the even more dreaded call home to the parents. That was the ultimate punishment back in those days.

You were in real trouble when the parents were called in. Back in those days parents backed up teachers, so a teacher's word about a student's conduct was taken at face value. The preferred punishment at my house was to get beaten across the backside by my father with a belt while lying face down on a bed. My mother never struck us but if we offended her, she would just refer us to our father.

"Just wait till your father gets home".

The worst part of this declaration was often in the waiting for it to happen. For instance, if it was summer vacation from school and your father was at work until 3 or 4 in the afternoon and you stupidly committed your crime early in the day, then you were subjected to the agony of having to wait all those hours until the inevitable showdown. It was like sweating out every minute on death row until they called you to the electric chair. If you were really desperate you might use the time to try to convince your mother to reconsider her referral but that rarely happened that I could recall. Maybe it was that dynamic that served as the deterrent (or maybe we were just smarter than the kids in the Bronx, although I have my doubts about that), but it seemed that most of our personal differences were settled off campus, usually after school hours.

That way there were, no teachers, no parents, no complications, and if you were the loser of the fight you took your beating and kept your mouth shut, if you were smart. And if you wanted that to be the end of it. Even the bullies respected that kind of fortitude. It was like an unspoken code of honor. The worst thing the loser could do was go home and squeal to his parents. Then the matter was likely to become a whole other thing with protracted taunting and bullying because the "code" between kids had been violated. Not only that but no one had any respect for a "squealer". That's just the way it was in that world.

When it came to adults and adult supervision, it was mostly a hands-off situation. Sure, there were little leagues and youth sports with the requisite adult oversight but that might only be one or two hours a week. As kids we got all the adult authority we could stand between school and home. To compensate, I believe we spent far more time than a lot of subsequent generations of kids engaged in interaction with each other. Just throw us a ball and that alone could keep us occupied and out of doors for countless hours. And to tell you the truth, I think a lot of our parents preferred it that way. Out of sight, out of mind.

Maybe my situation was unique in its composition, but I don't think so. I grew up in a veteran's subdivision and in many ways, it was kind of a social experiment in itself. When WWII was over, the government made ½ acre plots of land available to the veterans of the war. They came here approximately all at the same time after the war, built their houses and started their families. It was called the baby boom. Our subdivision was a four-road square loop, about a mile in its perimeter with about 170 to 200 houses in its embrace. There were around 30 to 40 kids my age and we all went to school together. There were probably 100 to 120 kids within 3 years of my age.

The subdivision itself was surrounded by farmland, woodlands, and ponds. It was like an oasis of humanity out in the countryside. Everybody knew everybody else and there was a lot of room for kids to play. And there was always someone to play with. And to get in trouble. There were two schools that serviced the area population. One was right at the mouth of the subdivision about a 10-minute walk from our houses and that one handled K-5 and the other was about a mile away and housed grades 6, 7 and 8. There was a high school also about a mile away but in the opposite direction of the junior high. That was our world growing up and the subdivision was the center of that world.

There were a couple of things we learned right away. The first was that our parents were not trying to be our friends. They were our parents first and as I said, they were more than likely to take a teacher's word over ours when it came to conduct, and they were more likely to support the word of the education system or law enforcement over ours. In a world of corporal punishment that did not make them our friend. To illustrate that, I just have to recall an event at a school dance.

In those days the legal drinking age in Canada was 21 but only 18 in the United States. The border was only 25 minutes from where we lived as the crow flies. We were only 15 years old but all we needed was someone with a license and a car and we were good to go. We knew some dives over there that would not card us and even if they did, we had fake I.D. It was referred to back then as "going over the river". We found a 16 year old that wanted to drive us and so we went "over the river" before going to the high school dance. We picked up a few beers for the trip home and we were in the parking lot of the high school finishing them off before we went in. We didn't even see the police car come up behind us until he turned his flashers on. We were busted. We had never been in trouble before with the police, so he decided to bring us to our homes. He put handcuffs on us (not so much because we were a danger to him) but I guess he wanted us to have the full criminal-on-the-way-to-the-big-house experience. It was past midnight by then. He parked his cruiser in the driveway of one of my friend's houses. There were no lights on, so they knocked on the front door. It took a few minutes but then the lights started coming on. The door opened, there was a moment of conversation, but we were parked too far away to overhear. The cop uncuffed my friend. The door closed and the officer came back to the car alone. We were just about to back out of the driveway, when the front door of the house flew open, and we heard loud screaming. We weren't parked too far away to hear that. What happened next seemed surrealistic. My friend came flying out the front door, with his father right behind him dressed in a housecoat and swinging a broom. They ran around the house into the backyard, and we could hear the whacks with the requisite scream after each one. The cop smiled as terror descended on my friend and me.

We went to my other friend's house next. His house was dark too. They knocked on the door. I was alone out in the cruiser, and I had thoughts of making a run for it. The scene was almost a replay of what had just taken place. The lights flickered on, there was a moment of muted conversation and my friend disappeared inside the house. The cop returned to the car alone but before we had a chance to leave there were screams that pierced the night and loud crashes of things being thrown inside the house and glass breaking. Another smile crossed the face of the cop.

If this had been today that same cop would have had to go back into that house and investigate for evidence of child abuse. But it was a time that parents were responsible for the discipline of their children and the police were not inclined to interfere. It was my turn next. I was trembling by this point. Shaking in my boots was more like it. To this day my friends never knew that I tried to cop a deal with the officer. I begged him, I pleaded with him to take me to jail instead of my home. I swore that I would never drink alcohol again if he would only lock me up. He wasn't buying it. That tells you all you need to know about how different things were from today. Imagine that a kid would prefer being locked up in jail with other criminals than being released into the custody of his parents.

The officer pulled into my driveway. Same set of circumstances. The house was dark. We knocked on the door and waited. No answer. We knocked again. No response. I couldn't understand it. My parents never went out. And they would have told me if they were planning to go somewhere at that time of night. The cop asked me,

"Are your parents not home?"

"I guess not I replied".

He tried the door, and it was unlocked. (No one locked their doors in those days.) He yelled

"Anyone home?"

Dead silence. He began unlocking the handcuffs.

"When your parents get home, I want you to tell them what you did tonight and that I will be back tomorrow to speak with them in person."

Then he left. I couldn't believe my luck. My parents never went out. If this had happened in the thousand nights before tonight or the thousand nights after this night, they would have answered that door. I found a note on the kitchen table that my brother was sick, and they had taken him to the hospital. I went to bed, but I didn't sleep. I heard them come home about a half hour later. I decided to wait until tomorrow to break the bad news about me. The next day was

Sunday. I was up early which was very unusual for me. I usually slept in a little later, but I was wrestling with a dilemma. To tell, or not to tell that was the question. What to do, what to do? I paced around all day playing out the scenarios in my mind. I came up with a plan that only a desperate 15-year-old mind could concoct. I would say nothing to my parents about what happened the previous night. I decided to roll the dice and bet that the cop would not return today as he said he would. I was going to call his bluff. But I had a plan B. I would hang out by the living room window and the second that I saw him pull into the driveway I would run to my parents and quickly confess. The logic (flawed as it was) was that if it wasn't a complete surprise and they had some warning of what I had done (last minute that it was) maybe it wouldn't go as bad for me. It made no sense, but I was grasping at straws at this point.

But what if he called? Same thing. I would answer the phone put him on hold and make a death row confession before he got to speak to them. I spent the whole day sitting by the front window looking at the driveway and answering the phone on the first ring. It was suspicious to say the least, but it was worth it. The visit and the phone call never came. The officer was banking on the fact that I would tell my parents (I would be too scared to defy his warning) and they would take care of the rest like they had in the case of my friends. He had underestimated the fear that parents instilled in their kids. And that's the moral of this story. The power that parents wielded back in the day.

I remember that my friends were grounded for a month, and they couldn't understand why I was not. Every once in a while, I would go and play in the street in front of their houses. I would see their wistful faces staring out the window as I frolicked blissfully and carefree like Snoopy the dog on their front lawn. Most of the time I pretended that I didn't know that they were watching (but of course I did). I didn't want to rub my good luck in their faces because I always had to remember that there was a cop out there somewhere with my name in his appointment book—an appointment that he had forgotten to keep—or had he?

In this same world that we grew up in there were no participation trophies. It was strictly meritocracy. Successes had to be earned. And there was no law against making your failures known as an incentive to do better in the future. That is relatively unheard of today. Unless you are a conservative or you forgot to wear your mask that day. In those instances, it is perfectly acceptable for a teacher to make a spectacle of a student in front of the rest of the class. In fact, I've heard of a recent instance in a NYC school where the class sang a song about their unvaccinated classmates who were soon going to be friendless, unless they were vaccinated. Kind of the in-person version of unfriending someone on the internet. Imagine that, nowadays you can be shamed in front of your peers for something that is not a decision you make. The teacher of that class is the one who should be ashamed.

But more on that subject later. By the same token we had a lot of freedom as kids and with that came responsibility. I remember eating breakfast on a Saturday morning and going out to play with nothing more than a bat and a ball, sometimes just a ball. That kept us occupied to lunch. Sometimes we came home for a sandwich, sometimes not. Then back for supper and outside again until the streetlights came on. That was the universal semaphore that it was time to go home for the day. Our parents might not know where we had been or what we had done all day and as long as we hit the assigned time stamps and didn't have any visible blood on us, we were in the clear.

It gave us the freedom to make our own way, find our niche in the world around us. It was a learning process that has been going on since the beginning of time—a veritable survival of the fittest. We learned that life and growing up was chocked with adversity and there was no escaping it. In order to deal with it you would have to learn to cope with it, mostly by your own devices. You learned to make friends and enemies and how to survive and how to excel. You learned your strengths and weaknesses because you were exposed to the elements, not coddled and protected like today where many adult supervised activities don't even keep score because they don't want kids on the losing team to be traumatized. Today everyone gets a trophy and as a result a kid does not get an honest assessment of his performance. He or she will later, maybe when they are in college competing for a scholarship and when they lose out and don't understand why, they will be unable to deal with such a disappointment and melt like a "snowflake".

The parents of today should shoulder most of the blame because they did their children no favors by not letting them discover the truth about themselves when they were younger. I remember as a student in my school system being awarded a silver dollar at the end of the year for having the best grade average among the boys in my class. I had worked hard to earn that award and I felt proud. I'm sure that it made some of my cohorts envious, but it also served as an inspiration to others. I also remember on the last day of school the teacher writing on the board not only the names of the silver dollar recipients but the names of the students who would not be promoted to the next grade. In that same moment you had students who were joyous and students who had their faces buried in their arms on top of their desks, sobbing. I have no doubt there was a lot of shame and even humiliation associated with that kind of recognition but as cruel as it might seem, it also could be an impetus of another kind. It could be a deterrent never to have that feeling of shame of failing a grade ever again. Today when a teacher is prohibited from marking the errors on a piece of work in red ink because it is too traumatic, posting the names of failing students would be considered unthinkable but back then that's the way it was.

Say what you want about the system back then, but at the very least when we graduated into high school we knew the basics of reading, writing and math. Things have deteriorated so much that a grade school education at the time is probably equivalent to a modern-day high school education.

At this point I thought I would defer to an assessment from a previous point of view.

Excerpt from SSTOP School Shooter Threat Onset Predictive

The Eggshell Analogy NEST-nurtured eggshell theory

To achieve its intent this work will follow a framework, of what I term NEST, the nurtured eggshell theory. This is a simple process that encompasses three premises. The first premise is that our society and culture is turning out over-protected, over-sensitive personalities (translated—pristine, unblemished eggs delivered from the nest) whose fragility is as delicate as an eggshell. The second premise is that they are ill-equipped to deal with stress (in particular the stressor of bullying in the school setting) and other pressures of life and each one has the potential to crack. The shell (which is the thin veneer represented by their individual coping skills) is their only protection against these stressors. Some will withstand the pressure, some won't. Think of it like a carton of eggs, with each egg being squeezed in turn. The third premise is that knowing a little information about the makeup of each egg before it is squeezed, will help us to determine which eggs are LIKELY to crack. And to achieve that end, we will use the application of a personality determinant known as the Myers-Briggs Type Indicator. Our modern society has incubated more eggs (potential candidates for cracking) than ever before. The question before us is, can we diagnose which ones are most likely to crack before we end up with a pile of broken eggshells?

The Absence of Adversity

There's no doubt that the world of today in which our children are growing up in is a vastly different place than the one that we, as their parents, experienced. That doesn't necessarily mean it is a better place, although we certainly hoped that it would be. Every parent wants their child to have it better than they themselves did. It is a noble premise indeed, but therein lies the problem. The pendulum may have swung too far. I came from a generation where we didn't have a lot of frills. All we needed was a ball and a stick and a little space and we could find a way to entertain ourselves for hours on end. We didn't need to be organized into a league with a lot of adult supervision. Our parents were the ones who had cut us loose for the day and we were quite capable of devising our own rules of the game. It wasn't perfect but we settled our own differences and parents rarely intervened. We learned to negotiate, compromise, argue, bully sometimes and even fight, to advance our viewpoint but it was all part of the education of personal interaction. Games were for fun, but they were also for competition. People played to win, to develop skills and to get better. One way to gain the respect of your peers was to be good at something. Competition fostered that esteem, built character, and helped us to stay in good physical condition.

Television was in its infancy at the time. Most households had one black and white, if they were lucky and programming was limited. I can remember many mornings staring at a test pattern, waiting for the network to run its Saturday morning slate of cartoons. Parents in that day would never have stood for allowing their kids to sit in front of a television all day. We were kicked outside, especially if it was a nice day. Many of us had jobs at an early age in life that would have precluded extended time in front of the set. And there were no remote controls. When your parents came home from work, they took control of the program selection. If you wanted to watch, you sat in the living room with them, kept quiet and watched what they watched. They paid for the set, so it was ludicrous to think that they were going to work all day and let their kids dictate what to watch. If you didn't like what they were watching. Tough. If you expressed your objections too loudly, you'd better watch out because you might get a cuff on the side of the head. This was an era where parental authority was rarely challenged, and corporal punishment was accepted. If you didn't want to be their remote-control system, you were better off going outside and playing. Television had its place, and it was not allowed to dominate your life.

Speaking of employment, I remember always working as a kid, as did most of my friends. Aside from the household chores of dish washing, taking out the garbage, cutting grass, and shoveling snow, for which you may or may not have been compensated, you might do similar services for other households in the neighborhood. Other jobs I held before I turned 16, included newspaper delivery, washing cars, house painting, working on a farm, picking fruit, pin setting at a bowling alley, babysitting and golf caddy. Since then, I have been a construction worker, tobacco picker, steel worker, factory and warehouse worker, salesman, fast food worker, truck driver, electronic technician, and educator. Having a job develops responsibility, work ethic and I always found that working at a job I didn't particularly like inspired me to find something better and acquire the skills necessary to get into that position. Having a job- built character.

Compare that to today when many of our children have never held a job. Some attribute that to the poor economic situation in recent years and that may be true to an extent. But the fact is that many of our youth feel that these menial jobs are beneath them. I had one employer tell me recently that

"I have openings—these young workers just don't want to get their hands dirty."

As a result, they have not developed any job skills. They don't know how to interview for a position, or interact appropriately with their boss and their co-workers, if they are hired. They are unwilling to work their way up the ladder. They don't want to deal with any adversity and as long as their parents are willing to provide them with all the comforts of home (food, shelter, a computer, and a television) there is no incentive for them to come out of their reality-insulated cocoons. I don't mean to get political, but this country is having a difficult time controlling illegal immigration. Historically, this is a problem that is diminished during times of high unemployment, but our youth, by their refusal to accept menial jobs and manual labor, has been responsible for providing unprecedented opportunities for that segment of our population. Some want to lay the blame at the feet of business owners but what's an employer to do when they can't find workers from the traditional sources.

In our time, there was no such thing as the internet. And the minute that you went out to play with your friends all your social skills were put to the test. You had to interact with real people and that meant being conversant, communicating and creating your own little niche in life, with an identity and its own strengths and weaknesses. It was a way to get information and to learn about life. Exposure to other people-built character.

Contrast that with the electronic world we live in now. Everything is at the touch of a finger. Most households have a color flat-screen television in every room with hundreds of channels via cable and satellite. Television is eminently available every minute of the day, with its generous offerings of gratuitous sex and violence and our children have had these electronic companions woven into the very fabric of their lives- at the expense of their physical and social development. Hollywood has supplanted the role of parents when it comes to dictating what morals and principles our children should have. Fake reality television shows substitute for real life and everybody wants the spotlight on them Everyone is carrying instant communication devices and cameras and they rarely look up from these devices even in the presence of others. I once saw two young people on a first date at a restaurant and neither one looked at each other or spoke—they were so absorbed in their electronic devices. And everyone wants to be noticed and if it can't be for something good, then something bad will do just as well.

The schools of our day were designed for learning. You learned basics, how to read and write add and subtract without electronic assistance. You did it in your head or on paper, you memorized, you learned to spell. The school didn't try to be the be-all-and-end-all of society's shortcomings. They were only one component of society. If you didn't comply with the rules, they could also use corporal punishment to get their point across. Teachers had earned a certain respect in the community and when they reported your misbehavior to your parents, it was a very rare day indeed if your parents chose to side with you. Schools of that day helped you to learn right from wrong and you could be singled out just as readily for something good that you did, as well as for something bad. That also built character. I remember a slogan from that time,

"What if you were judged by your actions when no one was watching?"

Schools taught not only morals, but love of one's country, civics, and civic pride. Good luck if you can find any of these being taught in a modern-day classroom. They have been replaced by Critical Race Theory, sexism and transgenderism.

The schools of today are forced into the roles that society has defaulted on. They are expected to be parents, babysitters, social centers, nutritionist, and doctor's offices, where everyone gets credit for trying and there is no need to correct papers with the trauma of red ink. Where vocational schools are almost non-existent, where no child is left behind, where helicopter parents sit in the classroom, and everyone goes to college. Incidentally it is being reported that parents are having a more difficult time than ever pushing their children out of the nest and off to college. Many colleges have established parent centers on campuses. Thirty and even twenty years ago this was unheard of. Parents want to hear from their child every day and some post the student's schedule at home, so they know where they are and what they are doing at all times of the day. Many colleges are reporting that they have to impose strict regulations to get these helicopter parents to leave the campus. Even when these drastic rules are imposed, parents have been observed spying on their child's activities with binoculars and telescopes. This is the culture we have created— where the United States ranks 1st in student self-esteem but 30th in academic achievement. Where a Massachusetts veteran high school teacher and the son of famous author David McCullough was recently castigated for trying to instill some reality into a graduation ceremony by telling a graduating class that they were no more special than all other graduating classes. Where the educational setting has become a more dangerous place than ever before.

The result of all this over protectiveness and coddling is that all the adversity has been removed. You get the trophy for just showing up. Electronic devices have eliminated the need for personal interaction. Without interaction there is no confrontation, no conflict—therefore no need to develop the skills to deal with these situations. We have scrubbed and sanitized the grit of life needed to develop personality, principles, morals and character. We have not prepared this generation for the ups and downs of life or given them the skills needed to cope with adversity. We have not represented the truth and as a result this generation is ill-equipped to handle it. What we have done is to deliver a nicely formed egg, with no cracks or dents onto the doorstep of college campuses and employers and now that fragility will be tested in the pressure cooker of life's storms. Whether our intentions were good or not, we have done this generation a disservice. And the impact will be felt by all of us."

What this is saying is that when many of our fragile children run their "snowflake bubbles" into reality and are burst, our children are unable to cope with that kind of adversity. Sometimes they lash out and take their frustrations on the rest of society— and some become school shooters.

It was a declaration that was warning us that school shootings were likely to increase. That prediction has come true as school shootings have increased, exponentially. But the impact is felt in all aspects of society.

It manifests itself in the oppressive nature of political correctness and the 'me too' movement. It is evident in "everybody gets a trophy" and elimination of competition, safe zones and spaces and the coddling and protecting of kids from every possible danger. It shows up in the neutralization of sexual identities and same sex marriages and gender-neutral bathrooms. It appears in open borders, socialistic tendencies, and lack of a work ethic. It is apparent in the decline of God in society and the removal of God in schools, the breakdown of families, increased homelessness, lawlessness, and mass shootings. Ironically it seems as if we are prohibited from disagreeing with anyone and yet we have never been more divisively in disagreement, than anyone can recall.

In addition to the "snowflake bubble", the leftists in conjunction with the perverted media, have created a mentality conducive to their purposes and an atmosphere of hate, also predisposed to their purposes. Foremost that have created a programmed voting bloc. All they had to say was conservatives are bad, bad, bad. Take our word for it. No need to investigate on your own. No need to find facts or rationale on your own and don't even question it. Accept it for its face value. We are telling you so it must be true. Especially since we will repeat it over and over again. *Only* three times a day—morning, noon, and night. So, go vote democratic and on the way to the voting booth don't forget to stop in at the school and thank your teachers, for us, for a job well done. But even that wasn't enough to win the 2016 election.

Then the mentality became to not accept the results of an election. Remember when everybody gets a trophy there are no losers. Except in real life there are winners and losers and losing an election has consequences. Sorry to burst your bubble but you don't get to run the country. Thank the media for deluding you."

When I was in school there was no social passing on or aging out back then either. I knew students who were ahead of me and who ended up in grades behind me. It was possible to fail a grade multiple times as compared to today where a student is apt to be passed on to the next grade whether or not he/she meets the requirements for graduation. It is why you have students graduating from high school without being able to read or write. In 2020 the Baltimore city school system spent over 16,000$ per student which was the third highest in the nation. What did the parents get for their money? Not much. At one high school 97% of the students were reading below grade level. At another high school one student passed only three classes in four years and graduated near the top of his class. These numbers are horrifyingly abysmal. And yet no one gets fired. Not the principal, not the teachers. This is what I refer to as a special kind of stupid. And what's even more shocking is that it is by design. That is the epiphany that is revealed in this book, and I remember that when I discovered it; it changed my world and everything that I thought I knew about it.

LEARNING THE ROPES

One of the most valuable lessons I ever learned from this atmosphere of always living on the edge of the next physical explosion, was that if you were to survive as a teacher, you had to show no fear. And it gets even gloomier than that. This was an atmosphere of constant threats, gangs, students threatening to commit suicide by jumping from third floor stairwells, fires being set in the school, students being subdued only with straitjackets and medication, physical altercations on a daily basis, not only student on student but student on teacher. Of rolling metal detectors, turning out guns and knives, and yet remarkably no one had actually been killed within the school building (there had been some killings on the streets and neighborhoods surrounding school). It was a running joke among the teachers that in order to get a permanent metal detector installed that, someone had to die within the confines of the school and that we needed a teacher to step up and volunteer themselves, so that our school could qualify. Oddly enough, there were no takers but all joking aside, this was an environment that was not to be taken lightly, in terms of life and death.

I know this is a terrible thing to say in this day and age but there's still a tremendous amount of racial hatred in this country. And what was even more surprising, is that it is so pervasive at such a young age. Students in the sixth and seventh grade have been taught by their parents to hate white people and this goes back several generations. I found myself in a situation where I had to be constantly wary, because in many instances, I was the only white person for miles around. The hatred I felt was palpable and undeniable. I was called every name imaginable, but I guess after a while, people can be conditioned to get used to anything.

I know this may sound like an overreaction to some people, but I literally had to confront the fact there was a possibility that I might actually die doing this job. I know it sounds crazy but until I actually acknowledged that realization I was operating under an atmosphere of constant fear. And I can tell you this, that if these students had even got a whiff that I was the least bit afraid, my teaching career would have been over in that instant—because they would've walked all over me. And in order to get into this state you almost had to pretend that you were like a soldier going into battle and accept the fact that you are going to get killed. Once you accepted that fact, the fear left you and you were actually able to function more effectively. I call this my dead man walking mentality.

I saw this principle at work first-hand with an Asian teacher who had come to our school. The Asian culture has a respect for education and teachers, that one would have to search high and low to find in the Bronx. Maybe he had the misconception that this was the way it would be in America or maybe he thought he could create that kind of atmosphere. Whatever he thought, his class wasn't buying into any of it and it was complete chaos with the inmates in control and this poor gentleman, literally cowering under his desk. Needless to say, it was the end of his teaching career in this country.

Another time the school had hired an African-American teacher over the summer. During the pre-school teacher workshops she was always describing how she had decorated the room with flowers and rainbows and was trying to create a positive atmosphere. I had my doubts about her sentiments, especially in a place like this, but I figured that she would have a better understanding of this culture than I ever would. Apparently not, because during her first class all the decorations had been ripped down and when she tried to reprimand a student, he had jumped onto her desk grabbed her by the neck and tried to choke her. She fled the school in terror, not even informing the principal that she was quitting. It was another demonstration of the law of the jungle and only the strongest survive but also of having expectations that are in tune with reality.

Then of course there were the verbal threats. Language in this school was especially crude. That was another difference between an inner city school and one in a rural environment. There was a student in the rural school that I taught that had had a behavior incident in a classroom and was removed from the premises by security. This student ended up in a counseling session and in the course of that confidential situation he indicated that he would like to kill the teacher. He was immediately remanded to a psychiatric hospital for a 2 week observation. In the Bronx, I was told several times a day, right to my face in no uncertain terms, that I was going to be killed. No matter how many times you wrote these incidents up nothing was ever done in the form of reprimands or punishment. This is one of the failings of the inner city school system, in my opinion. We have empowered the students to the point where their behavior has no consequences. It would not be tolerated in any other circumstance. If this same behavior were exhibited in a place of business it would lead to termination. If it was exhibited in a public place it would lead to arrest. Why are we allowing it in our schools? In fact had someone ever followed through on their threat and been successful, I am not sure that anything would've been done then. They probably would have just stuffed my body in a back closet with a broken computer and carried on as usual, although if that had been the case— they never would've gotten their permanent metal detector.

When I think back of all the years that I spent in this world of violence and intimidation and with all the threats that were directed at me, I can say that once I accepted the fact that I might die on this job, I can truly say that I was never afraid of any of my students, with the exception of one. In all those years, there were many students who were much larger physically than I was, there were many that were on medications that would make them act irrationally, there were many that were on drugs, there were many that were operating on hate and anger. But as I indicated with A's personality, I felt that they were open and straight forward in their intentions.

Towards the end of my time in the Bronx, I had a student coming to my class who was quite different than anything I had previously experienced. He was very small in stature but very intelligent. His personality could be described as oppositional and defiant. He was determined to defy anything that an authority figure declared, just to be defiant. If I said the sky was blue, he would say it was red, just to provoke the disagreement. He perceived everything that was directed towards him as criticism and personal persecution. And he never forgot one reprimand. It seemed like he stored them inside and let them fester.

He never once told me that he was going to kill me but he would just look at me with his black eyes—black with hatred, point two fingers at me and with the motion of his thumb, make like he was pulling the trigger on a gun. It was because of this student and his insidious nature, that I wondered how a kid could get to the point of coming to school with a gun and pulling the trigger on both students and teachers. I wondered what kind of escalation it would take. I wondered what kind of personality that kind of action would require and I wondered what kind of signs would be given. It was because of this student that I began this investigation which resulted in my Doctoral thesis—which ultimately became the centerpiece for a previous book. There was another joke going around the teacher's room, at the time that I was writing my thesis. That in order to prove if I was correct, the student would have to shoot me and then my hypothesis would be verified. I'm happy to report that it never came to that.

This brings up another important topic that is always very controversial—school shootings. When I was in school, we never had to worry about school shootings. We did have a shelter in place policy, but it was for nuclear attack. Back then we were told to hide under our desks and that was supposed to protect us. Even as children we realized that this was virtually useless.

Since then, schools haven't evolved all that much. Ever since the school shooting at Columbine High School in 1999 schools have been attempting to develop protocols to protect students from mass shootings. What they have come up with is basically shelter in place. Lock the classroom door, turn out the lights and hide in a corner of the classroom and be quiet. The object of this tactic is to fool the perpetrator into thinking that this is an empty classroom. There are many problems with this procedure.

First of all, if the attack occurs in the middle of a school day it is unlikely that these classrooms are going to be empty, and a school shooter knows this. A locked classroom door is not going to deter someone with a gun. Classroom doors typically have little windows to look in or out. It is virtually impossible to cram 35 students into one corner of the room and not be visible from someone in the hall looking through the window. Lots of schools use student issued personal computers for instruction.

One computer left running on a desk will give away the deception that this is an empty classroom. Students all have cell phones nowadays. One ringing cell phone will accomplish the same as a running desktop computer. Finally, do you realize how hard it is to keep 35 highly excitable students quiet especially in a time of high duress? If they hear one gunshot, I guarantee there will be screaming. Once the school shooter shoots out the lock on the door and gains entry the people in that classroom will be slaughtered like sheep.

There have been proposals for arming teachers. This proposal has been adopted in some states. Not every teacher has to have a gun. It could be one teacher on a hallway. If they volunteer, they could be trained in tactics and gun safety. I recall a high school that I taught in where my office was at the end of the hall with stairwells at both ends. I had a clear line of sight over both those entrances. Anyone trying to gain access to those classrooms on that hallway would have to go through my line of fire. I would have much preferred to go down with a fight than be led like lambs to slaughter. But then that's just me. Most liberals are horrified at even the mention of a teacher with a weapon.

Teachers' Unions and Tenure

In my time as a teacher I saw the good and the bad elements about both of these entities. One would think that perhaps I would be ambivalent about them. I am not. Despite the fact that I personally benefitted from both of them I am unequivocally against both.

It was about the time of my second year of teaching and coincidental with the arrival of a new principal in our school that the NYCDOE had undertaken a reform of sorts to its public schools. Schools were now to be graded on a letter grade system with A as the most proficient and F as deemed a failing school. A failing school was put on a two year probation status and if it could not correct its F grade in those two years it was designated for closure. In conjunction with this, principals and their salaries were directly tied to their school's performance.

And because principals were being held accountable for their school's performance in a way that they had not been previously they were granted unprecedented power to affect change. In fact it was as if the school had become their own private fiefdom and they were the absolute ruler over their domain and everyone in it. About the only obstacle in the path of their dictatorship was tenure and the teacher's union.

The teacher's union negotiated contracts, work conditions and in return collected dues from its members. It also held tremendous political clout. Paying dues to them was not mandatory but it reality it might has well have been. A teacher was harassed and ostracized if he/she did not contribute. I had never been in a union in my life and was basically told that becoming a member was absolutely essential if one wanted to have any kind of future in the teaching profession. That is what I desired so I complied.

In my first few years as a teacher, I saw my salary increase exponentially through the efforts of the union's negotiations for which I was eternally grateful. The teacher union is a great thing if you are a teacher. But that is ALL they care about. They claim that they care about students but don't believe it. All they care about is the teachers and collecting their dues. And they don't support conservatives. I soon found that out.

They were sending huge amounts of money to the Democrat Party. They were taking my money and contributing to causes and values that I was totally against and I had no say in the matter. In my last years as a teacher in the system I had refused to contribute and I paid a price but more on that later. My biggest objection to the teacher's union is that they keep a failing institution in place and it's never more evident than in the inner city. School after school is either failing or underachieving in this environment and the system is failing these students.

At the time charter schools were beginning to arise as an alternative to the public school system and they were beginning to achieve phenomenal results with the students. The teacher union saw this as an existential threat to them rather than a benefit to students and got legislation enacted that would block the expansion of charter schools. Their opposition to charter schools does a huge disservice to the students of minority parents. They are essentially trapped in a failed system.

The education system in this country could be dramatically improved if parents were allowed school choice. That element alone could have an immediate impact on the quality of education in the country and give millions of students and parents the hope they desperately seek. Simply by assigning education dollars to the individual and allowing them to spend those dollars on the school of their choice would open up a free market economy of competition and we would see the quality of education improve dramatically.

Our teacher unions do not care about what is best for children and that was never more exposed during covid. The masking, the school shutdowns, the remote learning. For the first time parents began to see what was going on in their child's classroom and they were appalled at what they saw. Critical Race Theory, inappropriate sexism and transgenderism and they rejected it out of hand. There was an exodus to home schooling to the tune of almost 30 %. The teacher unions in this country are the single greatest deterrent to a quality education in the United States and the single most important entity in the preservation of a failing status quo.

One of the greatest contributors to that failing status quo is a little tool in the toolbox of the union known as tenure. Tenure is akin to an apprenticeship in another profession or trade. The way it works in NYC is that a teacher auditions his skills and proficiency for three years during which time he or she can be fired by the principal for any or no reason and not have any recourse. After 3 years if a principal finds the performance of a teacher satisfactory they can grant them tenure.

Once a teacher is granted tenure it is very difficult to remove them from their position. It takes a documented regimen of incompetence and offenses to overturn a tenured status. Or an extremely egregious offense such as proven child molestation. Even in those cases an accused teacher has a right to due process and has to be found guilty. Tenure is not a guarantee of lifetime employment but it is about as close as one gets. In the case of a teacher running up against a principle who abuses their power it is about the only thing that protects the teacher. It is the only thing that limits the absolute power that a principal can bring to bear and it was the thing that saved my job for as long as it did.

While that is a positive in the defense of tenure, its negatives have far greater significance to the detriment of the education system. In many cases it protects the incompetence of the system by keeping bad teachers in place. Some of these teachers should never have been granted tenure in the first place but many just became that way after they were granted tenure. They became lazy and unmotivated and their classes suffered as a result. Pay raises and other incentives in the system are not based on merit but on longevity and so there is no incentive to perform. Tenure condemns the entire system to a level of mediocrity at best and complete and abject failure at worst. It should be replaced with a system of meritocracy that is more frequently employed by charter schools.

Taking It Personally.

There are a lot of bad teachers in the NYC school system and one of the main reasons for this is because many teachers take the behavior of their students, personally. Based on that belief, which is more often a false assumption, they react in ways that guarantees that a feud will result. In a situation where a student never gave a second thought that his/her behavior was directed toward a particular teacher, suddenly because of the immature reaction of a teacher it has become personal. Let me give you an example of how this works hypothetically, as well as anecdotally.

There are many broken families in this type of environment. Let's say we have an eighth grader, student B. His father has abandoned the family (as is often the case in the inner-city black community) and student B lives with his mother and grandmother.

Student B's mother is a substance abuser and didn't come home last night. He's not sure if she's just passed out somewhere or is dead. His grandmother is old so he has to pack a lunch for himself and his younger brother and get them ready for school. His younger brother tells him that he was bullied by a kid in the neighborhood and his skateboard was stolen. Something else that student B will have to deal with.

When B gets to school, he has a lot on his mind. He does not know for certain if his mother is even alive and she's really all he has. If she is dead his life will be upturned. He isn't sure where he and his brother will go to live and who will take care of them. On a lesser note, he has to play the role of parent and perhaps get into an altercation on his younger brother's behalf. He feels alone. Despair, hopelessness, helplessness, and anger even rage enter his thoughts.

He hates the world and everyone in it. He just needs the slightest excuse to lash out at anything or anyone, not so much out of hate but because everything that has happened to him since he woke up this morning has been out of his control. Taking his frustrations out on something or someone would be the first time all day that he has been able to assert some control over his life. Cursing someone out or punching them in the face would give him that satisfaction. So, he goes into English class in this frame of mind.

The class begins working on filling in the blanks in sentences with synonyms. He doesn't give a damn about synonyms. He doesn't give a damn about sentences that he will probably never utter in the whole of his life. His life is on the street and he knows how to talk to those people. The entire lesson has no relevance to what is happening in his life. He sees no reason to be here. The teacher calls on him and because he is not interested and has not been paying attention he calls her a bitch. She abruptly sends him down to detention. He doesn't care. He just wants to be left alone.

He sits down in detention and broods. He also doesn't learn anything. That's no skin off his teacher's nose. Student B's a troublemaker and he's right where he belongs as far as she is concerned, and she's not interested in finding out what might be behind his behavior. A grudge between the two develop. B's bad behavior in this class continues and he spends more time in detention during this period then he does in class. B fails English class.

Let's take the same character and set of circumstances and move it into my science class. I will admit that science might be the one subject that has a built-in advantage over some of the other subjects because of its hands on element. When the DOE made me a science teacher, I thought it was a curse, but it would turn out to be the biggest blessing of my teaching career.

Student B shows up in science class with a lot of troubles on his mind and in a bad mood. He is a time bomb looking for any excuse to set him off. Maybe he is so bent on a course of disruption that nothing can deter him. The kids are gathered around a lab desk conducting an experiment. He pushes the kid next to him, they get into a scuffle, and I have to send B down to detention. The difference is I don't hold a grudge against B, I don't consider him a troublemaker over one incident and I prefer that he be in the classroom.

Let's look at it another way. Suppose B arrives in the classroom and sees the class setting up the experiment. Everyone can participate if they choose. The experiment we are conducting today involves putting ice into a beaker, attaching a balloon to the mouth of the beaker, heating it over a hot plate and seeing what will happen.

There is interest on the part of the students. The students discuss the possibilities and make their predictions.

There is speculation. We begin the experiment. There is engagement. Even B's curiosity has gotten the better of him. He has forgotten his troubles at home for a few moments because he wants to see what happens with this silly experiment. Does he give a damn about the experiment? No. Does it have any more relevance to his life than the lesson on synonyms? Absolutely not. But is there more interest in the outcome? No doubt about it.

He wants to see what happens next in this crazy teacher's science class. He wants to see if the balloon will burst. But nothing is a foregone conclusion. Soon the ice melts into water and the water boils and turns into gas, the balloon fills up and bursts. Student B is not disappointed. Neither is the rest of the class. They think it's cool. (Believe it or not, one of the students in this class had his parents file a lawsuit against the school because he claimed that when the balloon burst—even though it was a predictable outcome that anyone could see coming from a mile away—it scared him so much that he fell out of his seat.)

What they don't realize is that they have just witnessed the three states of matter as it relates to H20. Liquid to solid to gas. They saw the solid state at 32° Fahrenheit and how much space it occupied and then the liquid as it melted and then boiled at 212° Fahrenheit and then the gas as it expanded filling the balloon to bursting. Whether consciously or subconsciously they have just learned that gas expands the most, then solid, then liquid. This is how learning in this environment occurs. You could say it is almost accidental.

I refer to it as controlled deliberate trickery, sorcery, wizardry, or PT Barnumism, whatever term you want to use. It was an effective formula and once I got the hang of it, trickery was my forte. I always said that I was never a born teacher but I never said that I wasn't a natural learner of some of the tricks of the trade. To me this was what it was all about, and I loved it, loved it, loved it.

Most teachers were satisfied with control of their classroom behavior and if any learning took place that was a bonus. That was never enough for me. If behavior was the be all end all why not just get a job in a prison? I knew these kids were capable of learning, but the key was in the presentation. Sure, they were a captive audience but that in itself does not guarantee a learning outcome. It was and still should be the teacher's responsibility to inspire that curiosity in them that makes them want to learn. That love of learning that a teacher can only hope stays with them for the rest of their lives.

Instead, bad teachers get bogged down in a morass of laziness and petty grudges that mires the whole system in a quicksand of failure and incompetence. To cap off my anecdote, Student B might have thought the science lesson had no relevance to his life until a time when he might have "borrowed" a bottle of beer from his mother's supply and hid it outside for later consumption. If it was in the winter when he returned to claim his prize he might have discovered that his bottle had frozen and burst because when liquid freezes it expands. Maybe he would have remembered that he learned that in Mr. Sneider's science class.

I think in the end a successful teacher is one who has a solid grasp of their subject material from multiple sources and exhibits an enthusiastic approach to presenting it, combined with equal doses of wizardry, sorcery, and PT Barnum. You can't force kids to learn. Even a captive audience does not guarantee that those students will learn. Not when we were in school, when I taught school and now. Probably more so now. And that's the crutch that an incompetent public education system with incompetent, unimaginative or lazy teachers relies on for results. That is one of the main reasons why it is failing so miserably. CNN appears to have a monopoly on all the televisions that are in the nation's airports. Essentially, they have a captive audience and that doesn't necessarily mean that people will watch their boring programming. Their plummeting ratings are evidence of that. A teacher can't bully students to learn. Fear only goes so far. It can make a class quiet as a mouse but not wise as an owl.

Mr. J

I remember taking a college course in the realm of my studies and it was entitled Classroom Engagement. Its purpose was to teach teachers how to increase all aspects of student engagement in their classrooms. From designing interesting lesson plans to methods of presentation and the logistics of delivery. I was amazed because the teacher who taught this class was the antithesis of the subject she was teaching. She taught in a low, monotone voice. She sat or stood by her desk in the front of the class like a statue. There was no emotion, no enthusiasm. Her droning monotone reflected her somber mood. At first, I thought it was a joke. I thought she was demonstrating how *not* to engage a classroom because she did an excellent job of that.

In contrast, Mr. J was one of the best teachers I ever had the privilege of observing. I think that it is imperative that all teachers get the chance to see how a competent teacher operates. This was a guy who did it right and it was a pleasure to watch him in action. He was the role model that I wanted to emulate. I had the good fortune of having one of my sped classes embedded into his eighth-grade history class for a semester.

He was amazing the way he circulated around a room and at one point or another during the lesson was in close physical proximity to every student in that room. There was lots of eye contact. And no matter where he was the lesson continued to flow. He made you feel like he was talking to you individually, only times thirty. He did nothing by accident. Everything he did was by design and served a purpose, but his presentation appeared so natural and unscripted. He mixed humor with serious emotion. He raised his voice, and he whispered. He acted out parts and he dressed for certain occasions. He showed lots of visuals and tapped into an array of teaching styles so that he touched a variation of learning styles. He was a whirling dervish of energy.

And that was the problem. It took a lot of energy to be Mr. J even for one class. It took an inordinate amount of endurance to replicate Mr. J day in and day out for the entire year. Not many teachers were willing to expend that kind of effort and energy. I was. I thought my students were entitled to that kind of effort. Unfortunately for Mr. J, he did not last very long in our school. No, he didn't burn himself out although that's quite common in the teaching profession.

He got himself in trouble because he was involved in an investigation of the Rubber Room component of the NYCDOE. I was never privy to the specifics of his situation, but he was drummed out of the school district. I learned that in exchange for leaving the system in the city he was allowed to become a paraprofessional where he had grown up in upstate New York, which was a different school district. Never again was he allowed to be a teacher in his home state. I heard he did that for a couple of years and then went to Europe where he was able to acquire teacher status again.

I lost a friend and a mentor, but the students of NYC lost one of the best educators they could ever hope to have. Replaced no doubt by a gay bubble-headed, leftist with purple hair, a nose ring, just out of college and with a rainbow flag hanging in their classroom in place of the stars and stripes. That's the way the system rolls. The students always come last. Just as under a leftist regime in the real world, America always comes last.

LIVING IN NYC

Living in the city was parallel to my teaching career and it is an entity unto itself. I would be remiss if I did not include some of the tribulations of trying to navigate life in the big city. They always tell you if you can make it here you can make it anywhere. What they don't tell you is that more often than not this place can grind you up and spit you out like raw hamburger.

New York City is a crowded place. It had always seemed that way. The first time I came to New York, I took the train. I had to take my special education certification test. I had already quit my tech job in New Hampshire and had made living arrangements in New York. I would be renting a room on the ninth floor of an old apartment building around 152nd street in Manhattan, near the George Washington Bridge and within walking distance of Yankee Stadium.

I had signed my 2-year contract with America Corps (Urban Teachers) to teach in NYC in exchange for subsidizing my licenses, guaranteeing me a job assignment, and funding my education courses. Everything was contingent on passing this test. No passing grade, no contract, no job. It was the only test being administered before the school year began. If I failed it, all my plans for the future would go up in smoke. Not to mention all the arrangements I had already made. I could not afford to put everything on hold for a whole year. It was now or never. I was taking a huge gamble. Talk about pressure. Failure was not an option.

I knew nothing about special education. But I had studied everything that I could get my hands on. I was ready to roll the dice. You know the outcome, otherwise you would not be reading about my teaching experiences in this book. It wasn't easy. I only passed by three points. Not exactly a margin of comfort. The point is I had made the trip to NY to take the test and finalize some matters. I had not driven my car because I had never been here before and did not want to have the added stress of driving.

I was totally on my own not knowing a single soul in this metropolis of 7 and 1\2 million people. It reminded me a lot of the time that my parents took me from a small town in Ontario and dropped me off at college in Boston. I didn't know a soul then and I almost hitchhiked back home. I was 17 back then and I remember crying before I decided to stay and give it a chance. It was the best decision that I ever made, and it completely changed the trajectory of my life.

Even though now I was almost 50 years old, the feelings were very similar to when I was standing outside that college dorm 33 years ago. I guess that is why we live life, so that we can learn from our decisions. I am proud to report that I did not cry this time although I have to admit I did feel like it but I had learned from that experience that this was another of those adventures that I was embarking on and so I should look forward to the journey.

But everywhere I went there were people. I recall that all I did on that trip was wait and wait and wait. In lines. Wait to get on the train, wait to go in a building, wait for the elevator, wait for the subway. I never felt so at the mercy of the elements, in my entire life. It almost cost me my future career. As I said, I had to be downtown around 23rd street to take the test needed for my certification. I had never ridden the subway in my life but I had directions from my landlord. I wrote them down and left in plenty of time to reach my destination.

I got on the subway, and it was morning rush hour. It seemed like chaos to me. I was trying to follow the stops on an electronic map at the front of the subway car but some of the lights were burnt out. It was ok because they weren't the stops I needed. The conductor was also announcing the stops over the intercom, but it was so distorted that you couldn't make out what he was saying. No one seemed to care. No one was paying any attention. They were all seasoned travelers. They knew where they were going. No doubt they had done it countless times, and this was just another day in their routine.

But I was a newbie. And I'm sure everyone else could tell. I was looking all around at everything. I was alert to every sound and everything that moved. One of the cardinal rules about riding a subway, no matter how crowded, is to never make eye contact. It is an invitation to trouble. It was very strange to me to see all these people crammed in like sardines in a can and everyone is looking down at the floor. Everyone except me. I was the duck out of water. No one said a word, but it was anything but quiet. The train rattled and rocked on the rail separations which in turn reverberated off the walls of the tunnels as we barreled through. It was a deafening cacophony of sound interrupted by periodic screeches of the conductors' unintelligible announcements.

We were moving along on time, and I kept checking my watch to make sure. Not only did I have to pass this test, but I also had to be on time to take it. If I was late I would be denied that opportunity. We were nearing my stop and everything seemed to be on schedule. We were one stop away when all of a sudden there was an announcement that I could not make out. I assumed it was the announcement for my stop. I got myself ready to exit. To my great horror the train went right by my stop without slowing down one iota. In fact, if anything, it was picking up speed. I was in a panic. What the hell was going on? I forced my way through the crowd to the door. I was yelling "Stop, I have to get off."

The people around me barely lifted their heads from their mile long stares at their feet. No one reacted to my panic or my plight. At best some displayed some apathetic amusement at the situation. The subway train blew by the next stop as well and showed no indication of slowing down. At this point I was almost apoplectic. Finally, a guy next to me responded,

"Hey buddy calm down. The train became an express. It will stop at 18th street."

That was my introduction to NYC subways and NYC itself. It's crowded, there is a lot of waiting and it is unpredictable. Things can change on a moment's notice. But why did it have to happen now? Why me? It's a mantra that I would repeat countless times in my years in the city, but it is something every New Yorker must contend with. It is something that you better get used to and learn to roll with the punches or you won't make it in the city. I got out on 18th street.

Problem was now I was on the wrong side of the tracks. I was on the downtown side of the tracks. I needed to get on the uptown side. You cannot just hop across the railbed to the other side. Either you will get hit by an oncoming train or you will get electrocuted by the third rail. I was so desperate I was considering that option anyway. I looked at my watch. I only had about 15 minutes to make my test. I could not afford to make any mistakes. How do I get across?

I spotted this strange formation further down the station. It was an overhead walkway. My heart was pounding away in my throat. I ran to it and got across to the uptown side of the tracks. Now I had to catch a train back to 23rd street. The first train whizzed by us without stopping. I only had 10 minutes left. I was on the verge of giving up. The next train was a local (I can say that now because I am an experienced subway commuter). It stopped. I got on. Somehow, we made it back to 23rd street and I made it to my test with about a minute to spare. This is why NYC wears you down constantly over time. It is why the saying came about "If you can make it here you can make it anywhere." I remember when I got home from this trip, the very first thing that I did was to get in my car and just drive out into the countryside. No traffic, no lines, no people, no waiting. I could just go. Freedom.

Of course when I went back to NYC for the start of the school year I drove and having a car presented a whole new set of problems. First of all the roads around the city are so congested that any minor disturbance such as a fender bender or a construction detour is enough to bring traffic to a standstill. I've seen just the mere fact that it started to rain cause major delays. And the drivers don't seem to know or care about the rules of the road. I once saw a driver cut across 4 lanes of traffic at 70 miles an hour without a blinker. The people in front of me who were slamming on their brakes produced a wall of red taillights. But then traffic congestion in a major US city is not going to be a surprise to anybody.

But the parking situation was a surprise, to me at least. Because everything revolved around the coveted parking space. I always said that to enjoy living in NYC you had to be rich. Rich enough to live on Park Avenue or the lower East Side, rich enough to go to the Hamptons for the summer but above all, rich enough to have your own garage. That was the gold standard for the privileged in my opinion. Then you can really enjoy all the attractions that NYC has to offer (and they are copious) without any of the common ordinary annoyances. Like trying to find a place to park your car. That seemingly trivial element becomes magnified in a city like NYC. I never realized that it would become such an issue.

I swear the city fathers set it up as a social experiment. The city designers said let's give the peasants one parking space for every 100 cars and let's see what happens. What happens is that the rats in the experiment fight to cram a car into anything that remotely resembles a parking space. They cut in front of each other to take a spot. They bang into the cars in front and behind them trying to squeeze an SUV into a space a Prius couldn't fit into. They argue, they give each other the finger, they curse, and they fight. Its road rage over a parking spot.

And if your car is one millimeter over the white parking line or 1 inch too close to a fire hydrant it's a minimum 100 dollar parking fine. I used to set aside 500$ just for the purpose of paying my parking fines for the school year. It was the cost of doing business in NYC. It was the job of the meter maids to raise revenue for the city as if they weren't already ripping you off with their eight- and ten-dollar tolls. In New Hampshire you got a smile and a thank you from the toll taker for your 1- or 2-dollar tolls. In New York you got a snarl and a sour puss face from another public servant who was overpaid and still hated their job and their life; but were too lazy to get out of the city.

I remember times where I would drive around my apartment for up to an hour looking for a spot to park and other times where I had to park a mile away. I can't tell you how many times I would park at night and not remember where I had parked the next morning and spend another hour looking for my car. Then there were the times where I got to the spot where I swear, I had left my car and I was getting ready to call it in for being stolen because it wasn't there where I thought it should have been.

And it got worse if there was some kind of event going on in the area because those people stole all of the normal parking spots. It was little things like this that you had to contend with living in the city and they beat you up every day.

Parking in the winter was a whole different animal. In the winter you were required to park on odd and even sides of the street on alternating days to allow for snow removal. If you forgot to move your car to the correct side of the street, it could be towed or booted. If you were lucky it was just another 100$ fine. Think about this though. By allowing parking on only one side of the street, the city had just eliminated half of the normally available parking spots. You'd have a hard time convincing me that we were not all part of some perverse social experiment. Someone was watching and saying

"Ok instead of a 100-1 ratio of cars to parking spots, let's double it and make it 200-1. And let's make it cold and then throw a foot of snow on everything and see what happens."

A snowstorm in NYC was the worst. For some reason the plows were always set up to dump the snow on the side of the street where the cars were parked. We used to get absolutely buried. It might take 4 or 5 hours to dig yourself out. And then people would get the idea that because they had put the time in to shovel out the parking spot that now they owned that section of the public city street. They would use all kinds of things to block it off or "reserve" it; everything from traffic cones to household furniture. I saw a guy put a couch in his space and sleep on it overnight. People were always getting into fights. It was crazy.

One of my best investments that I ever made was just before I went to work in NY, I purchased a Jeep Liberty. Not only was it compact enough to get into small parking spaces (and by the way by the time my tenure was over in NYC I was so good at parallel parking that if you gave me an inch on either side of my car, I could shoehorn it into a parking space without touching a bumper) but it had 4-wheel drive. When my car was buried, I just had to clear enough snow to get inside the vehicle and the 4-wheel drive would bust me out. What took others 4 hours of hard labor would only take me a matter of minutes.

Parking your car on a public street in a big city was not without its risks. It was always subject to dents and dings from fellow parkers, intentional acts of vandalism such as defacing and keying, break-ins and of course theft. I was fortunate enough that I never had my car stolen in all my years living in NY (which probably says more about the trade value of my car on the black market than anything else) but I did have it broken into on an almost regular basis. There was nothing really to steal except for some loose change and a CD now and then but even that was enough to induce a break-in. I learned that even some coins that could be seen from looking in the window was enticement enough.

I wouldn't have minded so much but these thieves never used a slim jim— a tool that unlocked a car door from the outside— they always resorted to smashing out my window. This left glass all over the place and an open window left the car vulnerable to weather and further vandalism. It was especially a pain in the ass in the cold winter months. In the beginning I would have to notify the insurance company and make an appointment with an installer and have it taken care of. This might be a few days, and, in the meantime, I had to drive around with plastic taped over the window.

Then someone told me about Fort Point. Fort Point was a kind of black market for just about anything. It was a very seedy section of the city—scary enough in full daylight but definitely not a place to be at night—and even more so if you were a white person. Whenever I had a broken window, I would take my car there. I would be directed to this unmarked building and in about a half an hour my window would be replaced, all the broken glass would be cleaned up and it would cost me 20$ cash and a five-dollar tip. No paperwork, no hassle and I would be on my way. At night it became an open market for drugs and prostitution. I think there was even a show about it made by HBO called the Hookers of Fort Point. It was a place where the entrepreneurial spirit was in full bloom if you weren't afraid to put your life at risk.

I rarely took my car downtown because the parking spaces there were even harder to come by. That and the traffic made it almost prohibitive. For those occasions I got to be quite proficient at riding the subways despite my initial introduction to this form of travel. The subway was in a lot of ways more dependable than the streets because on the streets you never knew what kind of surface traffic slowdowns you might run into. If there was a car accident you could be delayed indefinitely. But the subways ran underneath the streets and so traffic was not generally an issue.

The subway was a place where you saw every iteration of life in the big city. Sometimes the cars were so packed that you might be stacked like sardines in a can with complete strangers for the length of your trip. Talk about getting to know someone. With all this close contact going on I never understood why New York had such a bad reputation for being such an unfriendly place. Other times it might be quite isolated.

The one common denominator was the buskers and panhandlers. They were always passing through the cars looking for a handout. Most of the time they were ignored but some could be confrontational, and this would lead to skirmishes. Others provoked hostility from riders who just wanted to be left alone. Some of the street performers were actually quite talented and some could make a living on the street. But riding the subways always held the element of an underlying danger, at least for me.

There were always a lot of homeless and alcoholics and mentally challenged people on the subway. Some would just ride the system all day long for want of a place to go. It was especially hazardous at night. Many would be asleep or passed out on the bench seats. How someone could sleep on those noisy cars at the mercy of complete strangers was always a mystery to me. You always had to be wary of getting mugged or for a woman; raped. I saw derelicts defecate and urinate and vomit and spit on passengers on subway cars.

The subway stations were dangerous as well. There were always incidents of people falling or being pushed onto the tracks and getting hit by passing trains or getting electrocuted on the third rail. I saw a man riding a bike in a subway station (not sure what he was doing with a bike down there) fall over and crack his head on the concrete floor and no one stopped to help him. He was unconscious and bleeding all over the platform and all the commuters went around him. Some actually stepped over him. I saw a huge dead dog on a subway platform and same thing; people just stepped around or over it.

Sometime after 9/11, I was on a subway when a terrorist tried to explode a bomb in Times Square. For some reason it failed to detonate but at the exact time that it was supposed to explode, I was riding on a subway directly below Times Square. Who knows what kind of destruction he had planned. Something that always struck me every time I made the ride from the Bronx into Manhattan was how close but how isolated the two were. I would look out the windows of the train when it was on the elevated sections of the track and I would see the neighborhoods kept getting better and I would see less colored people on the streets. Of course, once I got into Manhattan there were hardly any colored people, and everything was so expensive. I realized that it was not the physical distance, it was the economics that kept the two separated.

There was no fence or wall, but it was like there was an invisible barrier and I used to marvel at the people in Manhattan who seemed so unaware; so unconcerned that just a mere 25 minutes down this track was a whole horde of people who hated their guts and many who would not think twice about killing them for what they had. Just another one of the anomalies of living in NYC, I guess.

There was an incident in which I happened to be walking in a neighborhood in Manhattan that was Malcom X territory. Apparently, he had preached and was killed in a church close by to where I was walking. It was around dusk and there were not many other people on the sidewalk when out of nowhere I was confronted by a group of black men all wearing dark uniforms.

I didn't know it at the time, but they belonged the Black Panther organization. It seemed like I was being selected for a test because they asked me what I thought of Malcom X. Given the situation, my reply might not have been the smartest thing I could have said in the interests of self-preservation but at least I was honest.

"I don't know that much about him," I replied, "but I can tell you a lot more about JFK."

I don't think that's what they wanted to hear because they closed in a little tighter around me and they were scowling.

When I told them that I was just a lone tourist who happened to be lost, I think it took them by surprise. I think they either sensed a trap and backed off or they couldn't believe that someone could be that stupid. I think they let me go because they thought I was TOO stupid to mug or beat up. It was a good thing they let me go when they did before I could tell them that I was alone, no one knew where I was or would know if I went missing, I had no next of kin, and I was carrying 2000 dollars in unmarked, untraceable bills in small denominations.

Another one of those anomalies was the time I witnessed a huge parade going down Broadway. I stood on the sidewalk watching and I soon realized it was a protest march for illegal aliens. It was apparent that a lot of the marchers were probably undocumented. There were an estimated 50,000 people in the parade, and most were carrying signs. They were trying to make the case to Americans that they should be granted amnesty. Actually it was a little more forceful than that. They were here illegally, and they were DEMANDING that they be given amnesty.

I gathered that from a few signs that were in English, but the irony of the whole situation was that all the speakers and chants and most of the signs were in Spanish. I guess they EXPECTED the rest of us who had come here legally to learn how to speak their language. There was always controversy over this issue and the authorities always contended that illegal aliens were too hard to find in order to enforce the law; catch them and deport them. Not on this day. There was 50,000 of them right in the street.

They could have herded them all on buses at the end of Broadway and had a caravan back to Mexico. If they had wanted. But that was never the goal because illegals were a thriving part of the city's economy. They supplied the labor for the rich and they owned businesses themselves. When I was living near the GW bridge I was in a section of the city that transitions from Harlem to the south and Spanish Harlem to the north. Many times, I would go into a store, or a bodega and the owners could not speak a word of English. I was always confounded as to how they expected to conduct business without knowing the language, but they didn't care about losing my sale. I was a small minority. They catered to the rest of the neighborhood which was all Spanish.

I didn't realize how important a segment of society illegal aliens are in New York City until I was invited to a symposium about obstacles to effective teaching. I was only a second-year teacher and was very flattered to be invited to this discussion with others who were professors and held doctorates and master's degrees.

On the topic of how we as teachers accommodate children of illegal aliens who are unable to learn because of the anxiety created by a life living in the shadows. I raised my hand. In my naiveté I suggested that the only way to alleviate the anxiety of being illegal might be to acquire legal documentation. Suddenly you could have heard a pin drop in that room. There was complete silence as all eyes turned to look at the person who had made such an absurd recommendation. Which happened to be me. No one said anything and my remark was patently ignored like it had never been said but from that moment forward I was marked as a racist. I was never again invited to one of those symposiums. Funny how that works.

I've probably painted a pretty negative picture of living in NYC and while there is that side; there is a lot of positive as well. The museums, the restaurants, the historical sights, and the entertainment, particularly the theatre venues are all world class in my opinion. The opportunities to observe and educate oneself are first rate. My job exposed me to many of these glorious venues and I did not take them for granted and they did not disappoint me.

I remember once I took a class on a field trip to the Museum of Modern Art. I was stunned at some of the world-famous art that was an arm's length away, the da Vinci's, the Rembrandt's and the Picasso's. I was mesmerized. Suddenly the spell was broken by a student who, almost oblivious to what was right in front of him, asked

"Can we go to McDonalds for lunch."

I could only think what a student from New Hampshire might give for an opportunity to visit a place like this but then again, no matter where you are from; at this age a kid's stomach is always going to be a priority. I went everywhere and did everything and that is the part of NYC that makes it one of the greatest places in the world. And there is always something happening-something to see.

It just so happened that the building that I lived in had a reputation at one time of being a renowned and respected piece of architecture. Over the years it had become out-dated and a little rundown but you could still detect the quality and the grandness underneath its tarnished veneer. My landlord who was in his eighties had moved in when it was under rent control and had lived there for many years, at a relative bargain. As the NYC real estate market took off, real estate became an extremely valuable commodity.

All the apartments in the building were being turned into million-dollar condos as soon as the rent control tenants left. Or died. Whenever we went out together, I always joked with my landlord that I did not want to walk too close to him because he was the only thing standing in the way of a real estate developer's million-dollar payoff.

But while I was there, our building was the location of a couple of movies. One movie, Salt starring Angelina Jolie was actually filmed on the floor that I lived on. In the movie there is a scene where she goes back to her apartment and a group of agents break in. I was allowed to sit right on the stairs in the hallway while they filmed that scene. There is another scene where Angelina Jolie appears to be walking on the ledge outside her apartment on the 11th floor. That was all an illusion. That was really filmed on the outside of the building but on the second floor and she was supported by all kinds of harnesses and guywires, that are edited out later. She was never in any danger, at least not in real life.

There was a cemetery next door to our building and those streets were used by the film American Gangster starring Denzel Washington and Russell Crowe. While it was exciting to watch some of the filming, I hated that movie because all the trucks and film equipment took up all of the parking spaces for us residents and every night, I had to park almost a mile away. "Law and Order" a series based in New York was always filming in that area as well.

I had my own little brush with fame during this time. I was interviewed on a cable station New York One on a show called the New Yorkers. They were interviewing me about a book I had written about Niagara Falls. It was a little bit of a jumble in my memory. I remember being nervous and I had a couple of drinks before going on the show, at a little bar across the street from the studio. I remember being in the green room with all the other guests before they called us out one at a time. (It really is a green room). I remember being in the room with Steven Seagal, who was there with his band and was going on just before me.

I remember going into the studio and the lights were so bright you couldn't see anything more than a couple of feet in front of you. I remember the host James Chladek wore a bright yellow sport coat (one that he wore for all his shows) and was in its own way his signature. I remember doing very well and making him laugh a couple of times and him inviting me back whenever I had another book or something interesting to talk about. It was late at night when I was done, and I took the subway back home. The show was aired live but the tape was looped and they played it all weekend. It helped me to sell my book.

I remember thinking that I was going to be a movie star and I was going to be rich. All the way home I had stars in my eyes. I got home late and had to be in school on just a couple hours sleep. I was a few minutes late. Talk about being brought back down to earth. When I got to my class they were in a state of chaos. Just a few hours ago I was a movie star and now I was looking at this. They were yelling and throwing things around the room. My paraprofessional (an older woman) was on the floor wrestling with one of the kids. Another kid was sticking his friend's head under the tap in the sink and running the water. I thought to myself

If I had film of what went on in this school people would not believe what they were getting for their tax dollars.

Now THAT would be an interesting topic to take on a talk show.

A couple of other things happened while I lived at this building. Yankee Stadium was a stone's throw away and there was one year where they were in the playoffs and the games were held at night during the school week. I was trying to get some sleep for work the next day and the Goodyear blimp was flying above the stadium and every time it did a loop it seemed like it was close enough to touch as it buzzed right by my bedroom window on the eleventh floor. It was keeping me awake and I was contemplating sticking a fork in it the next time it came by.

Also, while I lived there a plane captained by the now famous Sully Sullenberger just cleared the George Washington Bridge, when a bird strike took out his engines and he was forced to land on the Hudson River. He did it successfully and not a single person was hurt. I was at school when it happened but if I had been home I would have had a front seat to the whole thing.

Always something happening, some good some bad.

But always NYC's seamy underbelly is what tempers its greatness.

There was an event that happened that convinced me that I had to get out of New York even if everything else had been going great. I was in a crowded subway one evening during rush hour and there was a huge explosion in the tunnel. Of course, being after 9/11, the first thing that crossed everyone's mind was terrorist attack. The tunnel went dark and there was the smell of smoke everywhere. People were screaming and starting to panic. They started to push their way to the stairs leading up to the exits. It was a mad rush and the crowd was crushing people against the walls and underfoot. Some cursory emergency lights finally came on.

Then the ambulances came to the subway entrances as the people streamed out. Apparently it was not a terrorist attack but a transformer had blown. It had the same effect. I don't remember reading that anyone died but there were injuries. I made it out ok, but I vowed then and there that I had to get out of the city because I did not want to die in a dark, smoky subway somewhere underground with a crowd of strangers. I did not want that to be my final memory. If I was going to get killed I wanted it to be out in the open breathing fresh air and surrounded by blue skies, trees and mountains.

Once I had made the determination that, while New York was a great place to visit in terms of resources, such as world class museums and the like, it was not really a place where I would feel comfortable living—it was only a matter of time before I returned to New Hampshire. That time finally came in the summer of 2010 when I was hired to teach in a small school in the White Mountains of northern New Hampshire. Before I left New York, there was one last thing I wanted to do and that was to go to the top of the Empire State Building. It was an incredible experience—one that I will never forget. It was the most dramatic manifestation of the creativity and industry of man that I had ever encountered and that view is forever etched on the canvas of my mind. But as incredible as it was nevertheless it was a world of concrete and steel. A week later I was back in New Hampshire and one of the first things I wanted to do—something I had never done—was to climb a mountain. I did so just as the leaves were changing color and I felt like I was standing on the top of the world— only this was a natural world of indescribable serenity, sculpted by the hand of God.

Within weeks, I had gone from one extreme to the other.

THE MIDDLE YEARS: THE GOOD

I've always considered it a blessing that I was recruited to teach science, even though as I mentioned before, that I had no degree or even a license to teach that particular subject. Nevertheless, I went into it, full bore. I inherited a classroom that had nothing in it but bare shelves. That didn't last long. I used my own money to buy anything I could get my hands on. Supplies for experiments, games, art supplies, rockets, computer supplies, robotics and even various assorted animals, hamsters, birds, fish, ants and crabs.

I enrolled in the 'Globe Science Initiative' and earned classroom supplies through my participation with that organization. My intent was to turn those four bare walls into a living 'learn-atorium,' even though I was advised against it by my much more experienced colleagues, who said that it was a waste of time and money.

They said that these kids would never learn anyway, and in the end, since they had no respect for school, they would probably destroy everything in the room. I thought that I would give it a shot, regardless of what they said. There was no question that I was the rookie, but in this case, I wanted to trust my instincts and if it was the wrong thing to do, then at least I wanted to be proven wrong.

That became the day I learned never to listen to the already jaded, creative-thought-challenged, teacher union subsidized, veterans of the status quo.

Longevity does not equate to excellence in the classroom and probably denotes just the opposite. Because what happened in my science room was just the opposite of what they had predicted.

The kids adopted the animals in my room as if they were their own pets. They came in early before class to feed them and play with them. Instead of abusing the animals, they bonded in their respect for them and that expanded to include each other, something that might not have been there previously. I had LESS problems after I decided to go with this approach, even though I was in a position that was more vulnerable to misconduct. The potential for disaster was certainly in place.

Maybe it was because I had placed a lot of trust in the conduct of the students and they recognized that. For once they weren't being dictated to and they responded with kindness. In my room, they saw a reason to *come* to school. In fact, it was interesting, that for kids who were so dead set against school, all I had to say was that if there was misconduct, they would *not* be allowed further access to the animals. To them, the exclusion that they had previously so desired, all of a sudden became a punishment.

Not all of our animals survived their residency in my science classroom. We had a parakeet that the students absolutely loved. We would stock his feeder and cover up his cage when we went home for the weekend. One Monday morning I came in and uncovered his cage only to find him hanging upside down dead. He had unraveled a thread from his cage cover and had gotten entangled and hung himself. I always wondered if it was a suicide because of the environment that had been thrust into, but I'm sure it was an accident.

Another time we had a hamster who gave birth to a litter of eight. We separated the male, and I instructed the students not to touch the female and her babies until they were older. The kids followed it faithfully. Apparently, another class had used my room when we were on a field trip. We returned to a rather gruesome sight. Someone from the other class must have gone in the cage and got their scent on the baby hamsters because the mother had eaten the top halves of five of her own babies.

We even had an uninvited visitor to our classroom occasionally. This being the inner city, it was not a stranger to rats. We had our own guest rat—a rather large one I would guess—although I am no expert on rats. He would come out of the baseboard underneath the heating system and if a student spotted him there would be loud screaming until it (no doubt spooked by the level of noise) would scurry out of sight. There were plenty of other times when I was teaching class to an extra student because it would come out in the back of the class and just sit there quietly and observe. As long as the students didn't see it there was no disruption to the class. I like to think that it was interested in what we were learning.

At the end of each year, I donated the animals that had survived the ordeal. Some students requested that they be allowed to take an animal home as a pet. I was more than happy to oblige if their behavior had warranted such consideration and they had received permission from their parents.

I felt that this science room was an incubator of creativity, contrary to the regimental structure and the suffocating, suppressive attitude that was prevalent throughout the rest of the school. I am of the opinion, that creativity is on the highest level of a hierarchy that combines freedom and self- actualization. I think it was what the framers had in mind when they cast the phrase "pursuit of happiness", which is a direct result of having the freedom to be creative.

It was one of the reasons that I found teaching to be so fulfilling. There are always certain constraints in education that you cannot escape, but even within those confines, I often found myself in position to have great freedom to design and create a lesson of my own imagination. And to see it work as planned, and have the desired outcome, was the ultimate satisfaction.

This science room was that kind of island of creativity for these kids. And it became more so when I used it for the basis of my 'Hands-on Science' afterschool program. The first semester that I offered it, I only had two or three students enroll. It is amazing how word of mouth is transformative. By the second year, I had full enrollment and the program had to turn away students because of lack of room. The program director told me that my class was the most requested activity in the entire program.

I attribute that to the "trigger" theory. We had something of interest for everyone and we had no rules, other than to respect the property and their fellow classmates. These kids were free to create their own experience. We did so many things. We made colored 'slime' and sold it to raise money for school activities. We built and shot rockets in the school yard. We brought in all kinds of objects like printers and televisions and deconstructed them to see how they worked. You can't believe how educational and fun it is to take something apart.

I continued my work with the 'Teaching America's Story' program and the 'Globe Science Initiative.' These were independent programs that collaborated with teachers to make them better educators, by supplying them with information and materials that would improve their classrooms. In the course of my association with these organizations, I was able to secure thousands of dollars of grants, equipment and supplies for this title I school. I was the only teacher from my school that was an active participant in both these organizations, for the entire length of my tenure at this school.

One of the most treasured prizes, of working with these organizations was securing a mobile museum visit to your school. The Museum of Natural History (at great expense to them no doubt) had developed three mobile learning centers. These were huge mobile homes that had been converted into rolling exhibits. One was dedicated to dinosaurs, one to astronomy, (associated with the Hayden Planetarium and the famous astrophysicist Neil DeGrasse Tyson) and one was devoted to the study of marine biology.

These mobile units were sent out every week during the school year to schools and businesses to serve as teaching instruments and publicity purposes. To get one of these to visit your school for the day, was a real privilege and a feather in the cap of the host school. They park this huge monster in front of your school and the students see it when they arrive in the morning and classes get to take a tour through it. It creates a lot of buzz and excitement and even kids who hate school are curious to see what's inside. Everyone is on their best behavior that day. It is an event that makes the local news.

Typically, in any school special education students are on the bottom rung of the food chain. Most are mocked and suffer more social abuse than your average regular education student. In these instances when the mobile units visited, I was the one in charge of setting the schedule for the classes to go down and do their tour and I always made sure that my special education students got to do their tour first. It might have been the only day of the year where regular education students were envious of the special education students. It was gratifying to see the pride that my students walked around the school with that day like they were being seen as equals for once and they belonged to this school as much as anyone else.

Some schools have never ever gotten a visit from these vehicles. Ever. Some schools considered themselves extremely fortunate to have gotten one visit. I was able to qualify our school for three visits in three years, which is almost an unprecedented series of events. I was never given any recognition for this achievement by the administration of my school. Never even as much as a thank you. My reward for doing the best I could for my students was coming up. My principal had devised what he thought was a sure-fire way to bring about my demise. Just another day in the life of a conservative teacher.

Student C

By now I thought I had seen almost everything, but the case of student C stunned even me. Student C was a likeable 7th grader who was always getting into trouble. I was beginning to see a pattern. Student C was generally well behaved in class as long as we were doing visual or hands on activities. In fact he was enthusiastic about many of the lessons that I presented. He was also very well spoken in English. Even though he was Spanish American there was no hint of an accent.

However, any time that we were engaged in written activities such as reading or writing assignments, C would begin to get fidgety and start acting up in class. Many times I had to send him to detention and it seemed to me that that was by design. He never turned in any written assignments for grades. I teamed him up with another student to do a project and make a presentation to the class. C did it on his favorite subject—dinosaurs. There were lots of visuals of dinosaurs and written descriptions in his presentation to the rest of the class.

C did most of the talking and he knew the subject inside and out but every time a description was read, his partner did it. I had a hunch. As the next image of a dinosaur came up on the screen, C began talking about it in a knowledgeable way. When he was done, before his partner could read the caption, I asked C to do it. He kept trying to ad lib but I pressed him to read the caption exactly as it was written. He finally broke down and admitted to what most of the class already knew—that he couldn't read. I was stunned.

How had a student graduated to the 7th grade without being able to read hardly a word of English? And the amazing part— the part that had everybody fooled (his teacher's anyway) was that he could speak English fluently. It explained his bad behavior during class reading assignments. He was embarrassed that he couldn't read, and he was trying to cover it up. I immediately referred C to English remedial classes. His behavior in class improved dramatically from that point on.

Student D

Student D was another puzzling case until I figured out that he benefited from the "trigger theory". The trigger theory was not an official determination but something that I learned from my own experiences and observations. Student D was a very troubled kid. He was disruptive in class to the point that he had once tried to commit suicide by throwing himself down a 4th floor stair well. There were many times that he had to be removed in a strait jacket and once he had to be tied to a gurney and sedated before he could be taken out of the school in an ambulance.

D saw no purpose in school and frankly in life itself. Apparently, there was nothing for him in either one. The best a teacher could hope for with D was that he would sit there and be quiet for 40 minutes and then leave without incident. Of course he would never do any work or learn anything and he was failing all his classes. Maybe it was the work ethic in me but I just saw that to have this boy languishing like that was such a waste of his life and his potential. I had had some conversations with him and it seemed to me that he was fairly intelligent. I tried to bring it up with the school psychologist but the only thing he could shed light on was that D had a horrible home life. Apparently worse than all the rest of the kids who had horrible home lives as well.

It was almost by accident that D got "triggered." My science class that day was having an open period. Basically, there was no structured lesson, and I was allowing the class to explore anything that I had in my room. Some were playing and feeding the animals, some were using the Legos, others were engaged with computers. It was a free for all.

Some of the students were watching me. I was trying to put together some robots that I had just acquired from the Globe Science Program. Robotics was trending to be the next frontier and I wanted to incorporate that element into the science program. I had all the pieces spread out on my desk and I was struggling with the instructions on how to assemble them. Student D was one of the students watching me. Out of the blue D asked if he could help. D had never shown interest in anything and so I was more than happy to accommodate him.

Without looking at any of the instructions he set to work as if he had done this all his life. This was a fairly advanced and complicated piece of equipment and he assembled it with relative ease. And not only did D show an unprecedented amount of interest; he took control of the project. Once it was assembled he inserted the batteries and made it work. He was able to program it as well.

We dubbed our little creation "Robby" the robot. My class stood there open mouthed as D put the robot through its paces, making it go around the room, pick up objects and even do a dance. The robot became a centerpiece for the classroom that year and D became a star in the eyes of the other students. Not only did the rest of the class look at D though a different lens but D began to view himself in a different light.

He finally found something in school that he could relate to. School now had a purpose and he embraced it full on. He joined my afterschool with the express purpose of engaging with my robot. I noticed he began to take interest in some of the other elements. He loved going out into the school yard and firing our rocket. His interest in science expanded into the regular classroom. He began doing some of the work and he asked questions. The rest of the class was amazed. This was a D that no one had ever seen before.

Some of his other teachers reported that his behavior had improved in their classes as well. I would like to say that D became an "A" student and everyone lived happily ever after because of what happened in my classroom with the robot that day but that only happens in fairy tales. This was a gritty special education classroom in the inner city of Bronx, New York where such successes are in Humphrey Bogart's words "the stuff dreams are made of". Nevertheless, I feel that it is the job of a teacher to never stop trying to make those dreams happen.

Student D legitimately passed science class that year.

And to take the victories wherever we can get them. There is no such thing as too small.

Special Education Remedial Math

I've always felt that one of my personal accomplishments with students was one that did not win any awards. In fact, I got no recognition whatsoever other than the personal satisfaction of knowing what this group of kids was able to achieve. I was assigned to teach a group of six sixth grade students remedial math. They were imbedded in a regular sixth grade math class, but most were functioning on a fifth-grade level and a couple were 2 years behind.

The plan was to bring these students to the sixth-grade level by the end of the sixth-grade year. Once students fall behind like this it is very difficult to bring them back. You are essentially asking them to learn two years of math in one year and in the case of the 4th grade level students—three years in one year. That is a lot to digest in one year and a very big ask. Personally, I had my doubts that it could be done but luckily I was green enough to put my faith in the students and not jaded enough to accept the challenge.

So, I decided to take it one step at a time. I observed these students in the regular class setting. They were not engaged at all. The reason was that they did not understand what the teacher was talking about. She was miles ahead of their comprehension. They sat there pretending they were part of the class, but they never raised their hand, never participated, and would have been horrified if the teacher had ever called on one of them because they were totally lost. Any answer they would have given would have been laughed at by the rest of the class. In other words, they were too scared to learn and too embarrassed to expose how much they did not know.

They were like a shadow class—there—but not really there. The first thing that must be overcome particularly with special education students is their self-esteem or rather their lack thereof. In a cruel contrast of situations, regular education students are almost cultivated to have too much self-esteem. The coddling and the everyone-wins-a-trophy mentality produces a false sense of self-esteem. But Sped kids are the exception to this rule only in the opposite direction. Many are often told by their friends and even their family that they are too stupid to learn. Many of these kids believe what they have been repeatedly told and so that have little to no self-esteem.

My first task as their teacher if I was going to get them to learn anything was to convince them that they were capable of learning. We did that by drafting a pact amongst us that said we were in this together as a group. We would learn as a group and we swore to help each other out. We would start at the beginning and would not advance until everyone had mastered the previous lesson and was ready to move on. (This is not a method that I would recommend for all students, but I felt that it might be effective in this situation with this small group and their personality.)

To my way of thinking math was one of those subjects that was built on layers, and it was predicated on what came before. There were no stupid answers, there were no stupid questions. There would be no laughing at one's peers, no condescending or name calling. We were not going to be afraid to learn. And of course there would be plenty of incentives (candy for individual lessons and pizza at the end of the year) but they had to be earned. And we all signed it in blood. Just kidding, we used ketchup.

It was our version of the Mayflower Compact. I called it our Heinz Ketchup Pact. Because we were trying to "catch-up".

And so, we began. First things first. I started out with very simple exercises something that everyone could get right—in order to build up their self-confidence. They had to be convinced that they were not stupid—like they had been told all their lives. Day by day I could see their confidence level and their self-esteem increase with their small successes and their acquisition of knowledge.

Turns out this group was smarter than they had been given credit for. They had been given a bad rap and had been discarded and neglected because of it. They just needed some attention and some nurturing and some belief instilled in them and they did the rest. Their success inspired them to work harder. They progressed a lot quicker than I had thought possible.

About halfway through the year my group was still behind the regular class, but we had reached the beginning of the sixth-grade material. I noticed that my group had become part of the regular class not just SINO (students in name only). They were not afraid to ask questions and they did not display their previous panic when they were called on to give an answer.

By the end of the year the Sped class had caught up to the regular education class. The way that I knew was that one of my little Sped sixth graders had volunteered to go up to the board and explain a current lesson to the rest of the class. Something that they would never remotely have thought about doing at the beginning of the year. A special education student was leading the rest of the regular education students in solving a problem on the board—in effect teaching them. That told me that we had arrived. I was never so proud of a group of kids in my life. It was a testament to our commitment. I may have provided the environment and the culture that enabled the learning to take place but they had embraced the challenge and done the hard work to be successful.

No one gave us any awards for what we had done. But we knew what we had done.

And so did that regular education class.

We were flying high. The kids were learning and enjoying themselves while doing it, which is really the "dirty" little secret of education. If you can "disguise" learning in the "cloak" of a fun activity, you can "trick" your students into learning without them knowing it. We were learning, having fun and getting along as a group, with almost non-existent behavioral problems.

And then it all crashed and burned.

My conservative spots must have been showing.

Summary Of The Good

- Was contracted by Urban Teachers for 2 years pending certification
- Acquired my special education licenses and certifications.
- Was hired to teach science and assigned to the Bronx NY.
- Successfully taught one year of 7th grade science.
- Completed mentor program and was designated as a "keeper" by head of the science department.
- Volunteered for all extra-curricular administrative assignments and workshops for the school and the city/state such as marking examinations.
- Enrolled in a master's program for special education.
- Enrolled in the Globe Science Initiative
- Enrolled in Telling America's Story history program
- Was interviewed on New York One cable on "The New Yorkers" program
- Was accepted as a teacher in the after-school program to teach—

- Successfully taught 6th and 7th grade science.
- Volunteered for marking state examinations.
- Worked for National Endowment for the Arts Summer Program.
- Renewed my contract with Urban Teachers for another 2 years.
- Continued with my masters and history and science initiatives.
- Developed and taught a "Hands on Science" curriculum for the after-school program
- Started and ran the first school newspaper in the 55-year-old history of the school
- Successfully taught 7th and 8th grade science
- Worked for National Endowment for the Arts Summer Program.
- Completed master's degree in special education.
- Enrolled in master's program for psychology.
- Editor of the school newspaper
- Editor of the school yearbook.
- Was awarded a grant of lab equipment for excellence from the Globe Science initiative.
- Received the first ever in history visit to our school from the Museum of Natural History mobile unit for excellence in participation with the Globe Science Initiative.
- Became a mentor/ historian in the Telling America's Story history initiative.
- Was invited to a symposium of historians by the TAH initiative.
- Successfully taught Science and English.
- Successfully taught remedial math to 6th grade special education and had a 100 % pass rate.
- Worked for National Endowment for the Arts Summer Program.
- Completed my 2nd master's degree in psychology.
- Successfully taught 7th grade history with highest pass rate of all 7th grade classes.
- Received the second ever in history visit to our school from the Museum of Natural History mobile unit for excellence in participation with the Globe Science Initiative.

- Was awarded a grant of digital science equipment for excellence from the Globe Science initiative.
- Worked for National Endowment for the Arts Summer Program.
- Enrolled in my doctorate program in psychology
- Renewed my contract with Urban Teachers for another 2 years.
- Applied to National School Ambassadorship Program and was a finalist.
- Successfully taught 7th and 8th grade science
- Continued with science and history initiatives.
- Received the third ever in history visit to our school from the Museum of Natural History mobile unit for excellence in participation with the Globe Science Initiative.
- Was awarded a grant of robotic science equipment for excellence from the Globe Science initiative.
- Completed my doctorate in psychology. Had my thesis published.

THE TIDE TURNS

Although I never broadcast it, I'm sure my conservatism was showing in many little ways. How could it not? In the old days it would have been easier to keep under wraps because politics could be kept separate from the everyday trappings of life. But those days started to end with the election of Barack Obama. He was supposed to unite the country and he had a great opportunity to do just that but it was not a task that someone who had such a distaste for America was likely to undertake. Instead we became more divided than ever. This was about the time that if you disagreed with anything Obama proposed strictly on the merit of the policy itself you were labeled racist. And it expanded from there. For instance, if you supported the police, you were considered racist. And so, it became harder and harder to conceal one's conservatism when anything that you do or believe can be interpreted to be a political party affiliation.

I would never consider myself a political junkie by any means, but I've been following elections since I was a kid starting with JFK. I saw what happened with Nixon and Watergate. I lived through Carter and the gas lines and our defeats in foreign affairs and our loss of respect on the world stage. What is happening today is very reminiscent of what was happening to America during those Carter years. I witnessed an American revival in the Reagan years, the embarrassments of the Clinton years and the 9/11 entanglements of the Bush years. I believe that much of the corruption in government originated with Bill Clinton and continued through the Bush dynasty, but the real decline of America was precipitated by Barack Obama.

I believe that the difference between Barack Obama and all the other presidents was that while some of the others advocated for certain globalist principles to an extent, Obama was the first to fully embrace the complete agenda. While some of the others might have espoused policies that were not in America's best interests, they still loved the American republic. Obama was the first president that I felt did not love this country and was acting as a force from within to diminish it. It was as if he was from the leftist school of thought that espoused hatred for America and what it stood for.

I remember when Obama was elected. It was a big thing in the Bronx, as one would expect with its heavy concentration of black and Hispanic people. They were celebrating that America had elected its first black president and I was proud that my country had seen fit to overcome its racial prejudices in order to do that. However, my enthusiasm, soon waned.

Obama had come out of nowhere and was relative unknown on the national political stage. I think the media gave him a pass in their scrutiny of presidential candidates. In any event Obama was an unproven commodity. In that respect I wanted to reserve my judgement until I had seen him demonstrate some kind of a track record. For that I was called racist. Our principal who was white also, but much younger than I was ecstatic over Obama's election which told you everything you needed to know about his political ideology. He was high fiving the black teachers in the hallways. Our school was sending groups on field trips to Washington, DC to attend the inauguration. He held a rally in the auditorium for the whole school. During that rally I sat and politely clapped during the speeches and accolades that were being heaped on Obama. But because I wasn't doing cartwheels in the aisle a student asked me if I was a racist.

It was already beginning. An America that had just elected its first president of African American descent was being condemned as "systemically racist." A white teacher who was teaching in a school that was essentially all black was assumed to be racist because he was reserved in attitude. And if a white person criticized this president on purely policy issues, that confirmed it—he was a racist. They knew that we weren't really racists. It was just a leftist tactic to denigrate someone who disagreed with their ideas.

To me this was the beginning of our divisions in this country to the point where we have never been so divided as a nation. I thought Obama would use his historic election to alleviate some of the tensions in this country, but he seemed to throw gasoline on them instead. Nevertheless, this was a time when the liberals were in power, and they were spreading their wings. I only illustrate this because this was the world that I, as a conservative was trying to negotiate. In the end I had disagreed with and stood up to the regime in power. And it was ultimately responsible for my demise.

One other thing that I should point out at this time, because it speaks to another leftist tactic that had a direct bearing on my situation at the time. I will use a more current incident to illustrate this precept.

It involves one of the oldest laws of nature. It states that no one individual is more important than the good of the hive. Politically it means any individual will be sacrificed for the good of the party. In Orwellian terms, it dictates that no individual is irreplaceable no matter how important that think they are. In the reality of 1984, they are just an expendable cog in a machine, and it is the machine that must be protected at all costs.

This is not a foreign concept to the left—it is their doctrine and they have employed it before.

We see this playing out before our own eyes in recent events.

Presidential candidate Joe Biden was protected by the press and installed as president by the manipulations of a dishonest mainstream media. They withheld, distorted and suppressed information that would have negatively impacted Biden's campaign. It was information that should have been made available to the American voting public. In fact, three out of every seven Biden voters said they would not have voted for him if the truth about Biden and his son' Hunter had been known to them.

It was enough to get Biden elected and the democrats had their trojan horse that got them back into the White House. The democrats used Biden as a puppet to enact their globalist policies which proved to be unpopular and too radical for America. Biden had served his purpose but now he had to be jettisoned.

The evidence that Joe Bidens' usefulness had come to its conclusion was when the media that had lied for him began to turn on him. When CNN is admitting that The Hunter Biden laptop and inflation were now real when they had been denying its existence for years you knew Joe Biden's days were numbered.

There was a most amazing scene of Biden and Obama at an afterparty when Obama spoke on health care. Obama had a crowd around him including vice president Kamala Harris. Biden, president of the United States and the most powerful man in the world was left to wander around the room with nobody to talk to. Unbelievable. Then when he tried to interrupt Obama, he was totally ignored. No one turned to acknowledge him. He called out Barack's name. Obama ignored him. He put his hand on Obama's shoulder. Amazingly Obama continued to ignore him and kept on speaking with his group with Biden's hand on his shoulder the whole time. Even his own vice president never once turned to acknowledge him. If you could read their minds, it was like they were saying,

"Get away from us old man, don't bother us."

He had been rendered irrelevant. They gave their attention to the real power in the room. These people knew who the real boss was, and it wasn't Joe Biden. Joe Biden was being sacrificed on the altar of cancellation for the good of the party.

A fate I was about to experience firsthand.

In a world where liberals seem to be the majority in many professions it was not new for a conservative working in one of these fields to keep many of their views from public consumption if one wanted to continue their employment and the education system in NYC had definitely become a leftist domain. There was a time when the ratio of conservatives to liberals in education was 2 or 3 to 1. By the time I got there it was more like 30 to 1 and today it might be closer to 50 to 1. Anyways I wasn't there to espouse conservatism, I was there to teach kids to learn and I didn't believe that a teachers political bent should have a place in the classroom and I personally made a point of trying to stay as neutral and objective as I could. At least that's what I thought.

That being said I do believe that my tribulations were triggered by a single event and after this incident everything was different. Just to illustrate the contrast between before and after let me catalogue some of the before. In some ways I had become a darling of this school administration. My paperwork was always on time and up to date. My work ethic was unmatched as I showed up for work every day and on time. I volunteered for many extracurricular duties often working 12 hour days. I had shown an affinity for handling "difficult" students and I had shown an ability to get students to learn. I was being mentored by the head of the science department which was an honor in itself not every teacher experienced. He deemed that I was a "keeper" to the principal it became apparent that I was being groomed for greater responsibilities in the future.

I would be granted tenure and was finishing up my master's degree. I remember at about this time I had applied to an ambassador position for the following year and I had to get an approval from the office. My principal got wind of it and confronted me in the hallway one day that spring and was very disappointed in me. He stated that he had invested a lot of time and effort in my development and that he was counting on me for a significant contribution to the science department in the future.

My mentor (the current head of the science department) was retiring, and his successor was an older woman who only had a few years left before after her retirement also. Although he didn't come out and say it, he intimated that after the woman head of the department retired the position was practically mine for the taking. Naturally I was flattered to be thought of so highly as this was only my third year in the teaching profession. I told him that it was only a one-year position and because I was so new to the profession it was unlikely that I would be chosen anyway (which ultimately, I wasn't). He stated that he expected me to be back teaching science for him in the fall. I have to say that it felt really good to feel so wanted. I felt like my future in teaching never looked so bright. I felt like my principal and I were on the same page. This would be the apex of our good relationship. Never ever again would it be like this.

What happened was still inexplicable even as I recall it today. It didn't have to turn out this way in retrospect, but then again maybe it was inevitable. What precipitated our falling out was a single incident that was not in dispute, but each of us interpretated it differently perhaps because we were of different mindsets.

This is my written version of the actual incident report of that day.

Incident Report

It had been decided by a teacher vote that extended day would be held in the morning from 8am to 835 am. Special education teachers were to be assigned no more than 5 extended day students. Because other teachers were coming in late or calling in sick, I was asked by ——— the AP if it would be ok if I took some of the students who were drifting aimlessly in the hallways. He said that it would aid school safety. I agreed but the situation became increasingly non-compliant as more and more students were sent to my room. For many months I always had more than the required amount of 5 and there were days that I reached 22 or 23 students. When I brought this situation up I was told that it was still better to have these students under a teacher's supervision than out in the hall. I tried to be of assistance in the best interests of the school. But there is a reason that the number of students is restricted to 5 in the case of special education and that is because they require more attention. I could not give adequate attention to 23 students. As a result of this overcrowding and mixing of students who would not normally be placed in the same environment two students ——— and a girl half his size were verbally quarreling in the room. When they began to chase each other, I requested that they stop and I asked the girl to get her coat and go to her homeroom. There was no fighting. She was gone for about 5 minutes (plenty of time to get where she should have been) when I asked ———— to get his stuff and go to his homeroom as well) He left and closed the door behind him. Apparently, the girl had not gone where she was supposed to and was in the hallway when her and —— got into a further altercation. He threw her to the ground a couple of times like she was a rag doll. She fought back the only way she knew how and bit him on the arm. He ran screaming down the hall to security. She was arrested, cuffed and taken into custody and he had to go to the hospital for a tetanus shot and I was called onto the carpet for being the last teacher in contact with them. I was not aware of any of this because it did not happen in my room. While I was the last teacher of record the incident had been defused and the students were sent to their designated locations. I was accused of pushing a fight that had occurred in my room into the hallway. I was reprimanded and told that the parents of the students demanded that someone be held accountable and the principal decided that it would be me. A letter would be placed in my file. When I responded by saying that I did not agree with his assessment of the situation, and I would not be made a scapegoat and that I intended to grieve the matter which would result in an investigation of why the school was in non-compliance with special education regulations. I also stated that if I had gone months allowing my assigned students to roam the hallways during extended day I would have been disciplined. The principal grew very angry and threw me out of his office. He later decided against putting a letter in my file. I had won a battle of sorts. Little did I know that an all-out war against me was about to commence.

Even after the incident had been "resolved" in a manner determined by the principal. I did not hold a grudge. I felt I was entitled to my opinion, and I had made it known even if it was different than his. For me it was not personal and I felt I had a right to address my grievance with the union. It was basically a difference of opinion between two mature adults, and it did not have to end (what up until then had been a good working relationship), in my opinion. I've had difference of opinions with lots of people in my life and it didn't end the relationships. This is America after all, where we have the right to speak freely. I did not expect this altercation to be the end of the world, either. I soon found out how wrong I was.

My principal took it very personal. VERY personal. I guess he viewed himself as king of his little fiefdom and I had crossed a sacrilegious line of challenging the edict handed down from his majesty. And he declared war on me. Everything that preceded this event went out the window. I was marked for cancellation (even though that was not the term that was used in that day.)

In many ways I still don't understand why it has to be this way with liberals. Why can't a difference of opinion be aired out in a healthy discussion without name calling suppression and cancellation and even worse injected into the process? Especially in a nation founded on the constitution, free speech and democratic principles. Why do groups of people have to lose their rights when liberals have power? When Donald Trump was in power for 4 years not one liberal lost their right to assemble or speak freely. No one was cancelled or censored on Twitter or kicked off of Facebook. No one was labeled a domestic terrorist for expressing a dissenting opinion. All of these things and worse have occurred under Biden in just his first year. As a liberal or a democrat you may not have liked Trump but standing by idly and going along with these unconstitutional policies of Biden against half of your fellow Americans makes you as guilty and even complicit with these atrocities. Whatever your political affinity this is not right. Today these injustices are being visited on conservatives tomorrow they will include you liberals.

Just recently in Canada there was a trucker convoy protesting mask and vaccine mandates in Canada. The truckers ended up parking their rigs around the parliament buildings and blocking many of the streets. Other than that it was a peaceful protest. The Prime Minister Justin Trudeau refused to even meet with these peaceful protesters and instead labelled them domestic terrorists and white supremacists. He then invoked emergency powers which had never been used before to arrest the protesters, freeze their bank accounts, impound their trucks, seize their licenses, and fine them hundreds of thousands of dollars. Oh, and one more thing, if their pets became a responsibility of the government they would be euthanized.

All this because these truckers voiced a peaceful difference of opinion with the powers that be in a supposedly democratic society. The reason I bring this up is really to make an appeal to any liberals reading this. Many of you are pet owners. You love your pets dearly. The younger generations have even refrained from having children and instead replacing them with pets. Pets have become the new children of the family unit. I have personally witnessed many young parents treating their pets better than some of the children of my generation got treated. Imagine if your pet got taken away from you and killed because you expressed a difference of opinion with some politician. This is what is happening with these conservatives and leftists seem to be alright with it. You are going along with it because even if you feel that it is wrong you are not saying anything about it. Make no mistake it is wrong. Very wrong. And one day they will come for *your* pets. And then what. What's next? Will they take our children from us? Some say the public schools already have by means of their indoctrination which countermand the values of their parents.

The bottom line from this incident was that I had challenged the authority of the regime (the principal) in power. That was the real underlying reason for my persecution. I had not dutifully submitted and in their eyes, I was guilty of insubordination. Not only that but I was guilty of teaching my students critical thinking a sacrilegious contraindication to the leftist edict.

I was now expendable.

THE PERSECUTION: THE BAD

By this time, even though I had been granted tenure by my principal, my conservative principles had run afoul of his liberal agenda. It was around this point in time when he dedicated himself to running me out of the teaching profession. Every day I had to anticipate what attack might be coming and try to outwit this man, who had all the power in this domain. One thing you have to give liberals credit for if nothing else—they are dogged and relentless. And this was long before Trump Derangement Syndrome. In addition, to fighting them, I had to do the work necessary to educate my students.

Now I have a sense of what Donald Trump must have gone through each day as he fought the Democratic mission of impeachment in search of a crime and had to fight political opponents as well as the media and still do the work of trying to run the country. I will say that it takes an individual with an enormous amount of energy to withstand this kind of daily assault.

It was inevitable that in a system designed to produce conformity and stifle individual creativity, dominated by liberals, that an out-of-the-box conservative thinker would eventually get in trouble with the puppet masters. Never mind that the kids were thriving, because the one thing that you always have to remember, is that it is not really about the kids. They really don't care about the kids, even though they will tell you that they do.

I got in trouble because I ran contrary to the agenda. I didn't fit in with their narrative. It still amazes me that at one point, they thought that not only was I a good fit for this school, but that I was qualified to be offered tenure. All of a sudden, I didn't fit in their box. How could my teaching skills have deteriorated so quickly, when I should have been getting better? Truth be told, they weren't. I was the same teacher in terms of philosophy that I had always been. They just found out more about my politics and what they learned; they didn't like. In essence, I went through a version of what President Trump had gone through since his election, but this was long before the assault on Trump began. I could see the similarities. The end justifies the means. Liberals don't care about the kids if they can use them to get rid of someone they have targeted, just like democrats didn't care about the welfare of the country, (and folks that means all of us) in their quest to take down a president. (Trump) And they don't stop at just trying to get rid of you, they want to destroy you.

The machine was about to exact their pound of flesh for my insubordination. I had accomplished a lot in a remarkably short period of time but my fall was to be even more precipitous in an even shorter period of time. The first act of retribution was the cancellation of my afterschool class. I was told that they did not have the money to fund all of the afterschool activities. Somehow, my class, which had proven to be the most successful and popular, was the only one that was axed. After my program was cancelled, I remember coming back to my room from a meeting in another part of the school. There were kids lined up outside my room waiting to get in. I decided to defy the DOE and opened my room up even though I wouldn't be getting paid for my time. We flew under the radar for about a week until security was notified not to let students into my room and that effectively ended the afterschool program.

But the personal battle for the minds of the students was just beginning. I had been served notice. They were out to get me. I had no power and my only element of protection was that I had been granted tenure. The strength of that protection was about to be tested. Being a conservative in a liberal education system is a lot like being the roadrunner in a Wile Coyote cartoon. I know younger readers won't appreciate that comparison, but I know President Trump could identify. It means the liberal establishment keeps devising ways to trap you and get rid of you.

"But it is also true that some career officials...have sought ways to thwart Mr. Trump's aims by slow walking his orders, keeping information from him, leaking to reporters or enlisting allies in Congress to intervene." (New York Times)

Chuck Schumer said if you cross the left,

"They will come at you seven ways from Sunday."

The Class From Hell

One of the Department of Education policies or practices in New York was to separate disruptive learners. The philosophy behind this diffusion was one of, divide and conquer. There are many students in the inner-city school system that come to school only because the state law requires them to attend, until they are 16 years old. However, these students have no interest in school or learning and are there solely to be as disruptive as possible—derailing education for everyone.

For some reason school administrations feel it is more prudent to disperse these problematic students over many classes rather than concentrate them in one or two areas. The theory was that a couple of disruptive students could be more readily managed if they were diluted within a classroom, of say 30 kids, who were more disposed to learning. It was even felt that the majority of learners might provide a positive peer influence for the disruptors to conform. As good as it looked on paper, the opposite happened. In most cases, it only took one or two disruptors to destroy the learning atmosphere for the rest of the students in the classroom.

If you ask any teacher, it only takes one or two disruptive students to render the learning process almost impossible for the other students in the class. I have never understood why the school system feels it is necessary to sacrifice the education of 98% of their students while catering to the 2%. Administration's reluctance to remove these students is dangerous, in that it undermines the teacher's authority and it allows an aggressive situation to fester inside the classroom. The kind of behavior exhibited by these students would not be tolerated in any other area of life at home their parents would punish them, in the street they would be beaten up or arrested and on the job they would be fired—only in the schools does the system empower them to act with virtual impunity.

In my opinion, it came down to a simple case of math. Let's say you had 10 classes of 35 students each and 10 of the 350 were disruptive students. According to the practice of diffusion, one disruptive student would be assigned to each class. If it didn't work and all 10 students continued their disruptive behavior it could have a potential detrimental impact on 350 students. If you grouped all the disruptive students in one class—it allowed 340 to get their education and let's say by some miracle, the teacher of the 10 disruptive students was able to reach 3; the ratio of successful learning is 343/350. In anyone's logic, this was a much better ratio— although I can't imagine it would have been very enjoyable for the teacher, who had the one class from hell."

However, in a world of inclusion, no child left behind and non-discrimination, administrations are often reluctant to adopt the logical situation and this was always one reason, why the learning process was undermined in an inner city environment.

I was about to be the guinea pig in the next experiment. It was the next step in *my education* for being a non-conformist. My school had never adopted the all-the-bad-eggs-in-one-basket practice, at least no one could recall it being tried. Why don't we give it the acronym ATBEIOB, so we can lend some credibility to something that is just made up on the spot—like most of the other policies that the DOE comes up with. At least now, you and I can converse like *real* teachers do.

I was actually in agreement with the principle behind ATBEIOB, in that it afforded the highest percentage of students in the school the opportunity to be successful. That's what it was supposed to be all about, right, what was best for the kids and what was best for the school. It was setting yourself up to fail, (of course I was no stranger to that concept) with the knowledge that you would be sacrificing yourself for the good of the majority. Kind of noble, actually, when you look at it in that light but make no mistake, this was only designed to create a situation that would be so intolerable that I would resign. The quickest way to get a teacher with tenure out of the system was to make life so miserable that they walk away. This was the next sure-fire campaign that I would have to weather.

At the beginning of one of the semesters ATBEIOB was launched. The next morning I was staring into the sneering faces of twelve of the most disruptive, incorrigible kids in the school. Many of these kids were one step removed from serving time. It was like the Alcatraz of the prison system, where you send all your worst offenders. The police actually came into my room a couple of times while class was in session and took a student out in handcuffs. I guess it was the only place they could find him.

I knew just from looking at them that first morning, that it was going to be bad and, in retrospect, it certainly lived up to all expectations. I remember one student in particular—he seemed to have the eyes of a snake. Every time I looked his way, I felt that I was being stared at by a cobra. At the time, I was convinced that the administration had finally won. There was no way that I could survive this. But I was determined go down fighting and take it as far as I could.

It was a classic case of CLINO (classroom in name only). It was soon apparent that there would not even be the pretense of any learning taking place. It was for all intents and purposes, a holding cell.

The stress level was incredible, and I have to admit that I came close to cracking, on more than one occasion. I can say that now but at the time I tried to keep up the appearance that I was bearing up just fine. I don't think I was really fooling anyone because this was pure hell on wheels and everyone knew it, but in this war that I was engaged in with administration, I didn't want to give them the satisfaction that their plan was working.

There was one fly in the ointment with this whole scheme. I couldn't teach the whole curriculum to this class and other teachers had to be brought in. I had the class for 4 periods every day and 2 other teachers had them for 2 periods each. Because they didn't want this gang of hoodlums travelling very far down the halls, and wreaking their havoc during class changes, the two other classes they had to attend were adjacent to my classroom, one on either side.

I remember each morning before class began, all the teachers would stand in the hallway in front of their classroom doors. The principal would walk down the hall and greet each teacher before the bell rang, signaling the start of the day. I think he fancied himself to be some version of a military officer and we were lining up for inspection.

In my case, I think that it was more a case of checking on a patient with a terminal disease, to see how he was holding up. Every day, I smiled through gritted teeth but I never missed a day. In fact, I earned some extra bonuses in my pay, for perfect attendance. But I would be lying, if I said that I was coming through this unscathed.

It was right around this time that I noticed that my hands were beginning to shake. I had to get my students to do anything that required fine motors skills, for me. The ordeal was beginning to take its toll on others, as well. The two teachers on either side of me, were calling in sick more and more and this was putting a strain on the substitutes as well. Substitutes cost money and this negatively impacting the school budget.

In the end, the other two teachers were unable to cope with the CLH (class from hell) and they both resigned. I was also on the verge of doing the same. When no other teachers could be recruited as full-time replacements for the other two classrooms, the whole experiment was abandoned. I think by that point, half the class had been expelled or taken out in handcuffs anyway.

I recall the day, that the project was called off, standing in front of my classroom door as the principal made his rounds. I smiled back and saluted as he passed by, as the two locked doors of the abandoned classrooms on both sides of me spoke volumes. Then I stumbled from exhaustion into my room and closed the door. It wasn't until a full year after I had left New York, that my hands finally stopped trembling.

So, in the end I survived, mostly by default and attrition. Like the teacher unions always tried to drum into our heads, it's not how good a teacher you are, it's how good you are at hanging around.

But like the good leftists they are, they were not about to give up. They had only lost the battle, not the war. They had lost two good teachers in the process, but that was just collateral damage in the pursuit of their objective to get rid of me.

By this time, I had been removed as editor of the school newspaper.

I had also been relieved of my duties as editor of the school yearbook.

In fact, I had been suspended from all extracurricular activities. I found out about these the hard way. I was in the cafeteria ready to participate in state testing assessment when I was escorted out of the building in front of the whole assembly by two security guards at the direction of the principal.

These were just the opening volleys of the assault on my career.

Fan Incident

These students also had a strange ritual of fighting in the classroom. This was something that I had never witnessed in all my years of being student. I never saw two students have a physical fight in the classroom. This was a totally new phenomenon—in my day there were fights but these occurred after school or off school property, but never inside a classroom. The fights in the Bronx would often be preceded by another strange ritual of this jungle mentality and survival of the fittest regimen. In fact, it was almost as if it was a behavior learned from animals.

I had observed that many altercations were preceded by verbal sparring, that might include insults and name-calling. In many instances, this escalated into a physical confrontation in which the two students would come together, get into each other's face and butt shoulders, almost like two rams butting heads or horns. At this point, the confrontation could evolve into blows being thrown but I had also seen that the situation could defuse and both students could take their seats. It was as if they had proven that they were not afraid of each other and that they had a mutual respect for each other's courage. Apparently in the code of this jungle, there was no need to prove themselves further. You can find similar instances in nature when two animals confront each other and one submits and further physical domination is avoided.

Physical confrontation is a trait of both a crowded inner-city environment and poverty. Sometimes words are not enough to survive and one must take what one needs by physical force. Physical violence was an everyday concern in my time spent in the Bronx. Fights in the hallways produced a hurricane effect. The hallways at this school were very narrow to begin with and when you packed 1500 students (which by the way was the largest school I had ever been in until I got to college) into them they got even smaller. For some reason, many fights in the hallway started at lunch time and during the return to class a fight might start at the head of the hallway. You would then witness the hurricane effect, as it inevitably seemed to spin its way down the hall, constricted by the sheer number of students packed into a limited space.

Students were pushed aside and they in turn appeared to propel the perpetrators down the corridor. If there was an open classroom door, students were flung into that open space, It was really a phenomenon of physics, that I had never seen before. Another analogy is that of a rat being swallowed whole by a snake and watching the bulge making its way down the digestive track.

The classroom fight could be triggered by one student just looking at someone the wrong way. This produced an atmosphere of tension and always being on the edge. It was a cloud that always hung over our heads and you never knew when it was going to rain. The classroom fight could be a devastating event. Desks and other objects could be thrown around and innocent bystanders could be hurt in the melee. Often, other students were screaming and running out of the room and needless to say the lesson would be totally disrupted. Even once the perpetrators were removed, it would take time to put the room back in order and many times, even if this was accomplished it was almost impossible to get the students back to concentrating on the lesson at hand.

A classroom fight could have other devastating consequences. I certainly didn't escape the experience unscathed. I remember one hot day where the heat was also bringing tempers to the boiling point. We had an ancient relic of a fan that did its best to try and combat the heat but it was a losing battle, even for this ancient warrior.

It was a heavy, steel, floor model with a metal stand and metal blades and a metal protective cage. Suddenly two students exploded into a fight. After having exhorted them to refrain I got on the school's phone near the classroom door to call security, as was the school policy. In the meantime, one of the students actually picked up the spinning fan and tried to hit the other student over the head with it. He missed and the fan cage slammed into a desk. Apparently, the cage was a two-piece assembly and the front part fell off from the impact, leaving the spinning metal blades exposed. This didn't stop the student from trying to jam the fan blades into the face of the other student. When the others in the class saw the intended action, some of them ran out of the room screaming. I was on the phone, with my back turned to the class when one of the students slammed into me accidentally. I was hit full force from behind. My head snapped backward and I saw a spectrum of colors in one of my eyes, then it went black. I thought I had suffered some kind of temporary concussion from the impact, as there was no pain or any sign of injury associated with it, so for the time being I was concerned with more pressing matters. Such as the possible beheading of the student in my classroom. In the end, the only thing that saved the other student was that he had drifted far enough away from the wall plug so that the fan cord came out of the wall socket. Then security came and mopped up.

I went to the hospital to find out that I had suffered a detached retina in my left eye and was told at the time, that it was unlikely that I would ever see again as well as I had. Luckily for me, that initial diagnosis was proven wrong but only after six hours of surgery, two other procedures, months of rehabilitation, the insertion of a plastic lens, all done at New York Presbyterian Hospital, one of the best hospitals in the world at this kind of surgery, by the grace of God and a $60,000 hospital bill.

Outsmarting The Opposition

The next concoction that the principal devised to bring about my demise was quite devious in its concept. Having failed to bring me down with the most disruptive class experiment and having lost two other teachers in the process, he decided to try a different tact. His plan was to create a situation where my teaching incompetence would be evident and by providing supporting documentation (mostly fabricated) of that incompetence and additional evidence of insubordination he hoped to build enough of a case for my dismissal. The foundation of the case would be my incompetence as a teacher despite the fact that I had accrued no evidence of this in my first 4 years of teaching and the principal himself had deemed me worthy of tenure. In fact the opposite of this narrative was true. I had become a far better teacher with every year of experience. His plan was to design a situation where I was set up to fail.

It was decided that after 4 years of teaching science I would become a history teacher. And not just special education history but I would be assigned to a regular education class. In looking over my record he had discovered that my initial teaching license was in history but that I had never taught it. He was banking that my inexperience in this area would ultimately bring about my downfall. Also, my class number would rise from 12 students with a paraprofessional in the classroom to assist me to 35 students (which was the maximum allowed) with no additional assistance.

The next piece was even more ingenious on his part. He assigned me one of 6 6th grade classes that was moving into the 7th grade but had scored in the middle of the pack the previous year. In other words, the group he had chosen for me to teach were not the worst class in terms of achievement, but they weren't the best either. The thinking was that if he gave me the worst performing class it might be hard to demonstrate incompetence because even if I failed at raising their grades it could be argued that they were just performing at the same level as the year previous.

He did not want to give me the best performing class for the same reason because even though I might be incompetent as their instructor they might self-achieve and not expose my level of personal failure. The only way that would happen is if this class completely crashed and burned and that was not likely. No, he needed a class with an achievement level somewhere in the middle so there was plenty of room for them to underperform and that lack of achievement could be attributed to my ineptness. That would help make the principal's case against me.

The one fly in the ointment of this theory especially from my point of view was that with a class in the middle while it was true that there was room to fail, there was an equal amount of room to improve. The principal was not counting on this as an outcome. I was because I knew something that he did not. While I may have never formally taught history ever in my life, history was always my favorite subject. I was a history buff. I read all kinds of books and had visited many historical sites. I was currently enrolled in the "Teaching America's Story" program. I was particularly fascinated by American history and especially the Civil War. I would be teaching American history and the Civil War.

In the principal's mind he was setting me up to fail but he had inadvertently put my fate right in my own wheelhouse. I was confident that I would have the personal knowledge to teach this class. The only question was could I execute its presentation. I had decided that I was going to apply the hands-on principles that had worked so well with my science classes and see if they would translate into the teaching of history.

I put a lot of thought into devising lesson plans that were interactive. I put everything that I could adapt from my science classes into it. It was my greatest attempt at "trickery". We did a lot of role playing with props and costumes and hats. I had colleagues from my department assume characters and come in to speak. We did reenactments supported by lots of visuals. We incorporated elements such as the mousetrap game to build a lesson. Our crowning achievement was that we created and played out a kind of "empire trade" game of the English colonies built on the concept of the golden triangle of trade.

It was fun to play and proved to be such a successful learning tool that I was thinking of patenting it at one time. Other classes had heard about it and were actually asking me to play it with them in my after school program. Can you imagine kids who generally hate school asking you to conduct a class in their extra time? It was almost unprecedented. I believe that there is a version of this concept in digital gaming called "Forge of Empire". So much for my patent. Academically it might have been one of the most enjoyable years that I ever spent teaching students. I developed a template that year of materials and techniques that I would use to the end of my teaching career. But the principal was ready with plenty of tricks up his own sleeve.

The first thing they did was that they assigned me a different room from my home room to teach my history class and they made it the first period right after lunch. Then they denied me a key to that classroom. I know these might sound like superficial inconveniences but as anyone who has taught in that environment will tell you they were not insignificant.

My colleagues would attest that the first class after lunch is when the students are at their most restless. They are fully awake by now and may have ingested some calories and sugar for lunch and may have gone outside after eating. They may have got their blood flowing with some physical activities especially if it was a nice day. Now they are pumped up and raring to go and it is difficult to get them to sit still in any kind of a passive environment.

That's the first impediment a teacher must confront. Secondly by making me transfer classrooms I had to transport all my teaching materials to the other room. But without a key I could not get into the room before hand and set up so I would be ready to go when the class started. Without a key I had to stand in the hall with a restless class waiting for someone to open my classroom. The longer we waited the more restless the class got and that meant that they would even be more difficult to settle down and get into a learning mode.

This was done purposely to sabotage my lesson. I have no doubt in the least that it was intentional. And then once my class gained entry and got settled, they might have to wait for me to get my instructional materials ready which provided more opportunity for the class to be distracted. In a class period of 40 minutes in length, there were times that I was losing half of that instruction time waiting in the hall and getting ready to teach my lesson. Not exactly a fair and level playing field.

My protests naturally fell on deaf ears. The powers that be were going to do everything in their power to make sure I failed. And that was exactly the situation I found myself in. They had all the power, I had none. My career was at stake and the odds were purposely stacked against me. That became even more evident when the principal and his trained seal, who he referred to as his vice-principal began showing up to my classroom with random unannounced visits.

In those days we had to have our lesson plan approved by the office and then written on the board. Of course, because of the room transfer, I had to write mine on the board as soon as we were allowed into the room, which wasted more instruction time. And if I left anything out or deviated from what was written out on the board in my presentation (sometimes it was necessary to make adjustments during the lesson) I was written up. I was written up one time because one part of my lesson took 30 seconds longer to present than was indicated in the lesson plan.

A teacher was also judged on the behavior of their class. Teacher evaluations were done on a regular basis (twice a year) by the principal and his stooge, who he referred to as his vice principal. That year they were done much more frequently with my class. More evaluations, more opportunities to find things wrong and write up that teacher. Evaluations were always done during a single 40 minute period. Always.

In my case I had a double period one day a week with this class. Double periods were the worst. It was very hard for a teacher to keep a class engaged for 80 minutes especially in this environment. Of course this was the class that was selected for my evaluations and it was for the full 80 minute duration. I don't know exactly what it was but every time the principal and his storm trooper who he referred to as his vice-principal scheduled an evaluation for my 80-minute class my kids just seemed to be on their best behavior and there was nothing they could get me on.

It got so frustrating for them that they began to make up false evidence against me. "Fake news" as Trump might say. My prospects for having a successful outcome for the year were looking mighty bleak at this point in the proceedings. It looked like I was destined for a stay in the "rubber room" at the very least. For those of you who have no idea what I am talking about some explanation is required.

The "rubber room" was the infamous NYCDOE version of a Devil's Island penal colony reserved only for teachers. There have been a couple of documentaries done on the subject and it has been abolished since then. But the DOE in its infinite wisdom has created different iterations some of which are in existence now. The original version of the "rubber room" was a designated classroom usually in some school in your district. It served as a reporting station for any teacher that was on the fringes of the DOE. By that I mean any teacher that had run afoul of the rules governing conduct and employment.

For example, it might be that your school enrollment had gone down, classes were lower in number and as a result less teachers were required at your school, so some had to be released. This was what was called excessing. You were still a paid employee of the DOE but you were designated for reassignment. In other words, the DOE tried to find you a job somewhere else in their system for an arbitrary period of time (let's say 18 months). If they were unable to find you alternate employment or you refused their assignments, you were then terminated.

But in the meantime, you reported to the rubber room during the same hours that you would be present if you were teaching school. You signed in with the supervisor and you signed out when the school day was over(basically 8 hrs.). In the interim you sat at a student's desk in an unused classroom with fellow "rubber roomers" and passed the time as best you could.

Some supervisors allowed quiet conversation between the inmates but most wanted silence. You brought your lunch and ate it at your desk. You were allowed to go to the bathroom. You were not allowed to sleep. Some teachers worked on school related work others on personal matters. Most read books. Some just stared at the clock until it was time to go home. It didn't matter what you did because you weren't required to do anything other than to show up and remain quiet. All participants in the "rubber room" experience drew their full pay.

There were many teachers especially the veterans who regarded this as a paid vacation. No lessons to plan, no kids to deal with, no principals in their face equaled a lot less stress in their lives. I never quite saw it that way. I was a fairly new teacher and I wanted to learn all I could about my craft. I loved what I was doing and I was looking at the long term. I was starting out later than most teachers and I needed to get all the experience that I could. Maybe I was too ambitious (probably not a good trait for a teacher in a union). Sitting and rotting away in a rubber room was not exactly my idea of advancing one's career. Coming from the private sector, maybe I just had too much of a work ethic. I had been hired to teach and collecting a paycheck for *not* teaching was essentially stealing taxpayers hard earned money in my opinion.

You remained in this state of limbo day after day until your case or your situation was resolved one way or the other. Resolution could mean you were returned to the exact same situation that you had left—same school, same principal, same class, picking up where you had left off just like a paid leave of absence. In some cases, you might be reassigned, and, in some cases, you might be terminated, it depended on what you were in for and the outcome of your hearing.

In some cases, you were designated an ATR. ATR Absent Teacher Reserve is a term referring to teachers who are no longer appointed to a specific school but are reassigned to a school or number of schools within a school district or school system throughout the school year.

An ATR for whatever reason (misconduct or personnel logistics) has lost their position at their former school but they are still protected by tenure and are not eligible for termination. This assignment has taken many variations over the years. The main controversy about the rubber room model was that it paid teachers their full salary to do nothing but sit in a room. For most teachers who were just waiting reassignment, this was deemed an unnecessary waste of money. Like giving welfare money for doing nothing. Even welfare at times was reformed to include a work requirement in order to collect.

The DOE also incorporated some of these ideas and would require an ATR to perform some kind of duties rather than sit idly by. Most of the time it required teachers to work in school offices doing administrative or clerical tasks. At least the DOE felt like they were getting some bang for their buck However for some teachers this was not possible. Some teachers in the "rubber room" had been accused of sexual misconduct and were not allowed to be in contact with students until their case had been resolved in their favor.

A majority of these cases were accusations by a student against a teacher that usually (but not all of the time) proved to be false. Nevertheless the school always had to err on the side of the student. But over time the ATR situation evolved into a dumping ground for teachers who had fallen out of favor with the DOE and had lost their usefulness yet still retained tenure or seniority. Legally they could not be fired so the DOE devised a method that they could be assigned to permanent substitute teacher status and have to fill-in for absent regular classes.

If you have ever seen the behavior of classes when they are in the presence of a substitute teacher, you will understand what is occurring. The ATR is being subject to the worst behavior and before they can establish any kind of bond with a class they are then reassigned to another school, and they have to start all over. An ATR is relegated to dealing with the worst kind of behavior on a permanent basis and it is designed by the DOE to cause the ATR to quit. Few ATRs endure this kind of situation for very long no matter how much they are being paid. I made a personal vow that I would never allow myself to get dumped into a "rubber room" for an extended period of time. I kept that vow but only by the skin of my teeth.

I decided that it was time to start fighting back. I realized that even if I presented a perfect lesson under the conditions the principal had created they were still going to manufacture my failure. I had no power. My only option was to outsmart them. It was my only chance. I remember watching a scene from the movie Schindler's List. In this scene the inmates at a Nazi concentration camp were lined up and were being interrogated by the camp commander. Someone had stolen some food and the camp commander wanted the thief to step forward or be identified by one of his peers or he would shoot one person until the thief was revealed.

The first time he asked the question there was complete silence, so the camp commander picked out someone in the line at random and shot him. He asked the question again. At first there was silence but then a young boy stepped forward.

"Are you the thief?" the camp commander asked.

The young boy shook his head.

"Do you know who the thief is?"

The boy nodded in the affirmative.

"Point him out to me," the camp commander ordered.

The young boy pointed to the dead man lying on the ground who had just been shot.

When I watched this I thought it was so ingenious that the boy could think so quickly on his feet under such duress. It was this kind of thinking that was going to be required of me if I had any chance of surviving this full frontal assault by the principal.

I filed a grievance against the written charge that my lesson had not adhered to the timeline set by the principal. One section of my lesson had run 30 seconds over the time allotted. The regime got themselves in a little hot water over this one. Unbeknownst to me there was a little codicil to a lesson requirement that if the administration set guidelines for the lesson plans of their teachers, the administration had to demonstrate in a classroom situation that it could be accomplished, if challenged. In other words, in order for their written complaint against me to have standing, they were going to have to deliver my lesson within the allotted timeframe that they themselves had set.

The principal decided to delegate this task to the scholar he referred to as his vice-principle. I reveled in delight at the consternation that this was causing them. The vice-principal spent weeks rehearsing this one lesson; something that a teacher in the field would never have the time to do. Okay let that go.

On the day of the lesson presentation, the vice-principal, had all his materials set up well beforehand so that he was completely ready the minute the class arrived; something that I never had the good fortune to complete. Because they wouldn't allow me that luxury. Okay but let that go.

Then they brought in the best-behaved class they could find, and they had the principal and a paraprofessional in the room for support, elements that I was never able to enjoy. Even this supposed simulation was as rigged as it could be in their favor. Okay but let that go for now.

I took my own notes on the presentation as well as kept my own time checks on the lengths of each segment of the lesson. Despite the engineering of the optimal conditions the minion, often referred to as a vice- principal could not duplicate the lesson and timeline requirements that the administration was demanding of their staff. It was a pathetic performance and a dismal failure.

Not only was the written complaint against me dismissed but it was a victory for all the other teachers in the school. They no longer had to have their lessons restricted by timelines. In the future timelines could only be suggestions and overruns could not be used negatively in evaluations. It was a major blow to the principal. Now he was on the warpath.

I remember one instance that he had scheduled a class evaluation for me. Usually, a teacher would get a couple of these a year. Now that I was under the gun I was getting at least one a month that was announced and I could get others at random that were unannounced. Everything had to be perfect all the time or they would write me up. I was under a tremendous amount of stress.

Anyway, just before my evaluation as the classes were still in transition, the principal came in a few minutes early and saw that I had set up a mousetrap game and was planning to incorporate this into my lesson. He saw the kids arriving for the class and getting all excited and he knew that this was going to be a very successful lesson. I saw his face turn white when he realized this; and all of a sudden, he disappeared. The class got settled and I was about to start the lesson. Still no sign of the principal. A few minutes later I got a call on my classroom phone. It was the school secretary informing me that the principal was under the weather and would be unable to conduct my classroom evaluation that day. I couldn't stop chuckling over that one for the rest of the day. He had all the power, and yet *he* was the one running and hiding.

I decided to implement one other thing that was probably my sweetest victory and also had the greatest impact on the other teachers in the school. When the principal came into my room unannounced he would often sneak in sometimes even in the middle of a lesson sit at one of the desks at the back and start recording his observations on his forms. I was often taken by surprise, and I had no frame of reference for these visits. Often, they would just make up stuff that was incorrect or complete fabrications and it was difficult for me to refute without some evidence to back me up.

I bought a pack of inexpensive disposable video cameras. For every class that I taught I would give one to a student sitting in the front row. I instructed him or her to be at the ready to start filming. It was illegal to film special education students in class, but it was legal as long as the camera was only on me, the teacher.

Sure enough during one of my classes the weasel, sometimes referred to as a principal slinked in like the snake that he was and started his phony narrative disguised as a teacher evaluation. The student got my lesson down on tape and when I went to the teacher evaluation conference I was armed with the truth. I had time stamps, a record of what was written on the board and what I had actually said. I was able to refute his fabrications with concrete evidence. He was so embarrassed that he never did another unannounced evaluation in my room again. Not only that but when word got around to the other staff what I had done they began adopting this technique for themselves. I later learned that the principal was in a rage over this.

He was about to hate my guts even more. The semester was ending. The grade results of the classes were being tabulated. Out of the 6 7th grade classes my class had the highest grade average in the school. The other 5 classes were taught by veteran history teachers, and one was even taught by the head of the history department, and we had beaten them all with a rookie teacher at the helm. Additionally when the state history scores were announced seven 7th graders had scored 100 on the state exam. Five of the students had come from my class and only two from the other five classes combined.

At the student assembly where the students were given their recognition my name was not mentioned once. However, I had many teachers offering me congratulations, as well as the head of the history department and I was applauded at a Teaching America's History conference. The principal had gambled and lost. He bet my class with a middle of the road performance level would go down and he could blame it on me. Instead it went up to the highest level. I have to say it was one of the most satisfying achievements of my teaching career. Could it be that the principal was finally at his wits end? I was not so lucky.

Sexual Accusations

It was around this time that I got another scare, not because I had done anything wrong but because I thought that the principal would use the incident to his advantage in his crusade to ruin my career. The sexual component teaching in this environment was always prevalent. The students were sexually active far beyond the ages of kids in similar grades elsewhere. It's what they were obsessed with. They didn't recognize boundaries. It's what teachers had to constantly guard against. The cardinal rule for any teacher was to never be in a room alone with a student and have your door closed. It was an invitation to trouble.

If the student accused you of sexual misconduct in any way it was your word against theirs and if the investigation sided with the student, your teaching career was likely in jeopardy. Up to now I had never had a sexual allegation lodged against me. Now that I had a principal breathing down my neck looking for the slightest irregularity on my part that he could pounce on, it figured that it would happen.

It was near dismissal at the end of the day. The class was lining up near the door waiting for the dismissal bell. They started jostling and pushing up against the door and I asked them to move back because they were blocking the door and preventing it from being opened. They continued so I had to go over and get in front of the door and physically usher them back away from the door. There was some general contact but it was incidental and nothing direct or specific. I was just escorting a crowd away from the door.

The bell rang, I opened the door and the class left. Apparently there was a female who was one of the students at the front of the line. She went down to the office and filed a complaint against me alleging sexual touching. As I was in the office checking out for the day the principal came up to me with a big smile on his face and informed me of the allegation. Pending the investigation into the matter I was instructed to report to the rubber room the following day.

I was worried that this would turn out to be the albatross around my neck that would hang me. I knew that I was innocent, but I also knew that this could be manipulated to go against me especially with a hostile actor (the principal) conducting the investigation. It wouldn't be the first time and I'm sure it won't be the last.

I reported to the rubber room not knowing how long this would go with my fate hanging in the balance. Surprisingly at the end of my day I was instructed to report back to my school in the morning. Apparently I had been cleared of the accusation after only one day. Because it happened in the presence of the whole class there were plenty of witnesses. That still didn't guarantee an innocent verdict because my students could have conspired to lie and get rid of the white teacher.

But my students (right down to the last one) told the truth and corroborated my side of the story. The principal knew that with that many witnesses all telling the truth there was no way even he was going to be able to manufacture a false case against me and I was acquitted.

I had to admit I was holding my breath the whole time and it made me wonder that despite the tough exterior of these kids—could it be that they really did like me after all?

Insubordination

The first time I was cited for insubordination involved a mother and her children. Our school recently had three students enrolled, two boys and a girl. One of the boys was in my 7th grade class. All three had been previously home schooled. This was their first experience in a public school. The mother had done a fabulous job educating the three of them and they were all very smart. However, they were sorely lacking in social skills. They were painfully shy and totally naive and trusting.

Every day they were heckled, harassed and bullied by the other students. They were being conned out of their personal possessions or they were being stolen out right. Every morning they would come to school well dressed and groomed with lunches in hand and by the end of the school day they looked like they had been mugged. Empty handed and totally disheveled.

The mother was paying the school a visit to see what was happening and she wanted to speak to each of her children's teachers. The principal wanted to keep these students in our school even though he had not put a single measure in place to ease their transition. It was a case of naked Darwinism—survival of the fittest. The principal instructed all of us teachers not to say anything derogatory about the school to the mother. It was obvious he was going to give her a snow job and her kids would continue to suffer.

When she spoke to me, I could see in her eyes that she was desperate, and she was pleading for someone to tell her the truth. I decided that even though it meant going against the principal's directive I was not going to lie to this woman. I told her that academically her kids would be fine in any school. I told her that in my opinion her kids were being completely overwhelmed by the social aspect of this public school. This school was a tough place by any standard and the students here could be as cruel as anywhere.

I told her that maybe she should look into a parochial school or a charter school, at least until her children got their feet on the ground.

Apparently, she took my advice because a few days after her visit she withdrew all three of her children from our school. The principal was not too happy.

A while later I had confided what I suspected had happened to a colleague of mine. He was the only one I had ever told. I had trusted him. His name was DB, and you will read about him in greater detail later in this book. It wasn't long after that I was confronted by the principal about my conversation with this mother. Although I never admitted to any wrongdoing I was written up for insubordination and a letter went into my permanent personnel file.

The second time I was brought up on charges of insubordination was a little more serious.

There was a time when the UFT (United Federation of Teachers) changed its stance on school fights. In previous years it had required teachers to break up fights and physically separate the combatants.

This policy resulted in a lot of teachers being injured in the line of duty and plenty of lost man hours. The new policy stated that a teacher was only required to inject themselves into a physical altercation if one student was being so overwhelmed by the other that there was a concern for their well being. It seemed rather vague and subject to a lot of interpretation. I welcomed any reprieve especially after suffering a detached retina in a previous incident.

One afternoon an incident erupted in my classroom in which a student triggered by something in the room grabbed hold of a metal rod that was part of a display stand and started swinging it like a baseball bat at the front of the room. The students did the requisite screaming and exited their desks and retreated to the back of the room. The boy was at the front of the room visibly upset and cursing loudly. But up to this point he had struck no one and did not seem to be targeting anyone in particular. He only swung the metal bar if anyone approached him.

As long as we maintained our distance, he was not a threat. I called security and the class waited for their arrival. They were better equipped to disarm the situation. All of a sudden, our new vice principal popped into the room. I guessed the old one had washed out because this time the principal had chosen a woman to be his flunky. I'm not sure what her motivations were or what she hoped to accomplish but it was no secret that I was a marked man.

She ordered me to approach the boy and remove the steel bar from his possession. I explained to her that the boy would swing the bar at anyone who got into his proximity. At present he was not an immediate threat and security was on its way, should be there any minute. The wise thing to do was to remain calm and wait. She would have none of it and ordered me to get the metal bar once again. I refused outright.

Her response was "Are you going to leave it to a woman to do your job?"

I replied, "No I don't think anyone needs to put themselves at risk."

She was determined to do this. As she approached the boy, she stuck out her hand to point at the boy. She was holding a walkie talkie and it came inside the radius of the metal bar. The boy swung the bar, hit her on the wrist causing her to scream and sending the walkie talkie skittering across the floor. She grabbed her wrist and moved back out of range just as two security guards arrived. They disarmed the boy without further incident and escorted him down to the office. The vice-principal earned a trip to the hospital with a broken wrist.

I would have liked to have said "See I told you so" but I never got the chance. I was written up for insubordination and that earned me another trip to the rubber room. In what was yet another surprise I only spent one day there again because it was determined that my actions were in line with UFT policy.

Summary Of Persecutions

- Cancelled my afterschool program
- Removed me as editor from the school newspaper
- Removed me as editor from the school yearbook
- Physically removed from testing assessments.
- Prohibited from participation in any extracurricular activities on school property.
- Assigned the Class from hell.
- Subjected to constant unannounced classroom visit and surveillance
- Subjected to numerous teacher evaluations.
- Assigned Seventh grade History class without proper license
- Assigned Special education remedial class.
- Suffered through incident with fan because of inadequate discipline procedures.
- Subjected to sexual accusation
- Designated to rubber room for disciplinary action

- Designated for rubber room for disciplinary action, insubordination.
- Tried to excess me had have me classified as an ATR (teacher reserve list)
- After 16 satisfactory teacher evaluations I was given 12 consecutive unsatisfactory ratings which became part of my permanent record
- Released derogatory confidential job performance evaluations instead of job verification information even after I had left the NYCDOE system.

TRAPPED LIKE A RAT

After having endured over a year of the principal's harassments it was apparent that I had no future in this school as long as he was in charge. And it didn't look like he was going anywhere soon. Little did I know it at this time, but it wasn't just my tenure in the school that was in jeopardy, it was my job in the profession. I had decided that it was in the best interests of all concerned it I found employment elsewhere. I put together my resume and I began sending it out to other schools in NYC as well as applying for other positions that were advertised. I figured with my years of experience, my accomplishments and the high need for special education teachers in this environment, it would be fairly easy to secure a position in another school.

I went to plenty of interviews and had positive reviews from my interviewers, but I never got any call backs, or any job offers. I was suspicious and I suspected it had something to do with my principal. But I couldn't figure out why. He wanted me gone and I was obliging. One of my prospective employers told me what was happening but only in strict confidentiality. My principal had one upped me. Because he had given me Unsatisfactory ratings in my teacher evaluations, it was a requirement that any school that was interested in hiring me had to get approval from the principal. And when an interested school would contact him about hiring me, he would sabotage my chances by imparting negative information about me. I couldn't believe it. He was actually *preventing* me from leaving.

I went to his office for a face to face. He said that leaving his school was not sufficient, but he wanted to get me out of teaching altogether. He would settle for nothing less than my resignation from the system. I refused his offer.

There are many times in my life where I have felt that I was in the presence of evil. Sometimes it's a particular place, sometimes it's a person. Looking into his eyes at that moment when he said that he would be satisfied with nothing less than the destruction of my career (when he knew that I was a competent teacher and that I had the potential to help a lot of kids) I saw the pure hatred and I saw him for what he was—real evil. The mask was off. I have to admit it sent chills down my spine. There was no doubt what I was up against. It was the same evil embedded in the teacher's unions when they say that the interests of the children, they serve come first but then they deny school choice when they know that would really benefit children. In reality it is the preservation of their power that comes first. It is the same evil that is embodied by the democrat party when they are willing to bring about the destruction of their country in order to preserve their control and their power. It is pure unadulterated evil. I was going to have to fight like I had never fought before. And pray.

I sent the following letter to the principal's office.

Letter to Principal

It has recently come to my attention that the only information an administration official of a school is permitted to release about one of its teachers to prospective employers is attendance related matters. This is in direct opposition to what you personally stated to me when I informed you of my intent to apply for alternative employment-even when injecting your input was not required by the prospective employer.

Your statement to me was to the effect that you had checked with your legal department and that you felt that it was your responsibility to inform a prospective employer of my performance rating situation at ——————.

Since I had applied to other schools and since we believe this to be incorrect and a violation of my rights, there is an investigation into the matter. If evidence is discovered that you provided employers with negative information on my behalf, and that a hiring decision was impacted, yourself, the city, and the DOE will be implicated in a lawsuit.

It did stop him from releasing negative information about me to prospective employers, but it did not stop him from denying my request for a transfer. Because of the U rating he had given me he had the power to veto a transfer to another venue without giving a reason.

There was a hearing scheduled with the NYCDOE to adjudicate this whole matter. My only chance was to convince the DOE that I was being railroaded. If I could prevail over the principal at this hearing, I could overturn my U rating and I would be free to seek employment without having to go through the principal.

I prepared my case and what follows are some excerpts from that hearing. The entire transcript can be found in Appendix C.

Hearing

Aside from my student teaching I had never taught before and despite this lack of experience, training, and content knowledge I achieved 4 years of satisfactory performance reviews (3 under the current administration). If you consider that to be an average of 3 formal observations a year and a year-end assessment grade, that equals 16 straight out of 16 assessment opportunities that a satisfactory grade was achieved.

In addition, I was also granted tenure by this principal.

Point Of Reference

In the spring of —— there was an altercation (see incident report) that involved extended day students. The end result of that incident was that Principal——— and I disagreed over the proposed course of action He intended to reprimand me and put a letter in my file. The meeting was attended by ——— who was the UFT representative at the time (see report notes). I indicated to Mr. ———— that if a letter was put in my file that I would grieve the incident and the resulting investigation would reveal that there were more students in my room than was allowed by special education regulations. He decided against placing a letter in my file.

I contend that this is the reference point and the crux of the unsatisfactory performance ratings that were to follow and continue up until the present time.

My Side

Barely a month after the aforementioned incident in ——— Principal ———— attempted to excess me (see grievance report) even though I had seniority over other teachers in the school. This was barely 10 months after he granted me tenure because as he stated I was a valuable addition to the school and a keeper and had assigned Mr.——— a recently retired veteran science teacher to advise me.

His contention now was that I was out of license (which I had been from the beginning) and advised me not to contest it with the reasoning that being an ATR was a "good situation". Of course, I contested it with the UFT (documentation should be on file) and spent the summer with no specific assignment and being listed on the ATR list.

I reported to work in the fall of———and Principal ——— gave me a program the day before school started, apparently realizing that he was unlikely to prevail in an excess hearing. I was given a room and assigned to teach special education social studies, although this was still not my appointed license area.

The room was a disaster (it took two weeks of intense work for myself and a paraprofessional to make it presentable) and I was never given any social studies textbooks. On Sept 11 (only the second week of school) I was observed and given an unsatisfactory review on the basis that my lesson did not follow the textbook material, even though I had no textbooks to work with. Subsequently, (a few months into the school year) some old tattered soft covered texts were discovered in a closet and have been utilized but there is only 7 of these for 29 students, clearly an inadequate supply. (See example)

It was the first unsatisfactory observation I had received in my entire time in the school (and has been followed by a litany of the same) and was the trigger point for justification in subjecting me to a constant pattern of scrutiny, observation, meetings, and lesson plan criticism, all under the facade of offering "assistance".

It is my contention that this was never the intent of this principal and his administration but rather to find any incident of non-compliance that could be written up and placed in my file and when none were available, they were not above construing events to fit their circumstances in portraying me in an unfavorable light. Considering that in the first 4 years of my employment not one letter was placed in my file and the number in the last **12 months alone, is around 2 dozen, one might imply a pattern of excessive harassment.**

If the general assumption of any reasonable person is that a teacher generally improves his professional skills and expertise in the classroom through experience, exposure to models of excellence and continued professional development and content knowledge, one would reasonably have to assume that I am a more accomplished professional now than I was in my first 4 years.

I have now failed every formal and informal observation since the incident of —— (6/6 U ratings after going 16/16 S ratings.) How did I suddenly become an incompetent classroom teacher who in the beginning of my career could do no wrong and now cannot do anything right?

I contend that this illusion is a contrived one that exists only in the eyes of this administration.

It was an impression created and perpetrated by a coerced and compromised administration led by a principal jaundiced by an obsession with retribution for a teacher who stood up for what he thought was morally and professionally right.

In the spring of —— I was offered the opportunity to have my inevitable U rating changed to a satisfactory rating if I agreed to resign from the NYC education system. I declined.

Evidentiary Defense

In addition to my presentation of my own viewpoint with respect to specific occurrences and the refuting of specific allegations, I offer the following evidence in my defense.

Of all the professionals in-house and outside of the school who were in my room for observations or consultation, including Mr. —— and his wife who was a consultant for the DOE, Mr. ——— head of the SS dept, Mr. ——— head of the Sped dept, ———— OSEI consultant and Mr. —— AP of Sped, the ONLY negative references I received regarding my academic presentations were from this principal and his administration (and only after the incident of————)

To this day I have never been provided with a model of instruction from this administration despite repeated requests to this effect.

How is it that my lessons were repeatedly condemned for being unsatisfactory when during the observations the students were engaged, well behaved for the most part and produced the desired results from their efforts, as my paraprofessionals in the room can attest?

How is it that my lesson plans were repeatedly condemned for lack of academic rigor, especially one I submitted about the presidential inauguration and yet that same lesson was incorporated by Ms. —————head of the English Language Arts department and presented to the entire school as an inauguration assignment during the inauguration day proceedings. (See lesson plan)

How is it that my model of the Revolutionary War "trade game" became an example for other teachers in the social studies department to teach the events leading up to the Declaration of Independence and is being proposed for professional development by the head of the social studies department Mr. ———.

How is it that I was the ONLY teacher to have both my lesson plans accepted by the TAH program as models for teachers in all the districts that they represent and is on their current website available to all teachers everywhere? These were lessons that had to be demonstrated in front of peers who had achieved PhD and master's level academic achievement at ——— University. (See website printout)

How is it that in previous years other teachers were sent to my science labs to observe my methods of hands-on instruction? I would cite a previous evaluation from Mr.—— to the effect that –when it comes to hands-on instruction Mr. Sneider may be one of the best in the building.

To this day I have never been supplied with an adequate number of the required social studies textbooks for either of my 7th or 8th grade classes, despite repeated requests for compliance. The response from the administration is that it is not our responsibility. However, if my lesson plans are to be developed and the curriculum adhered to, based on the materials that are provided to the students and that supply is inadequate for instructional purposes, then how can that be the criteria for the purposes of observation and evaluation? It is my contention that if materials on which performance is to be judged cannot be provided, then the criteria itself is rendered invalid.

How is it that through my continued participation in professional development programs such as TAH and Globe Science and being placed in a content area that is my field of expertise that I have become a less accomplished educator than I was in my first year?

If my methods of instruction and adherence to the POEM model (lesson plan) were apparently unfailingly delivered in a satisfactory manner during my first four years of teaching, how is it that when the only thing that changes in that equation is the content area—and the content area is now enhanced because it is the field of expertise by way of a bachelor's degree, subsequent certification and continued professional development—how is it possible for that instruction to deteriorate to a level considered unsatisfactory?

This would seem to run contrary to common sense and conventional logic unless one realizes that this has been a contrived and concerted effort to undermine the efforts of a teacher who has always put the education of his students first, has strived for excellence in the classroom as well as trying to improve the learning environment of the school, has always presented himself as a role model and conducted himself in a professional manner.

This continues to the present in which I have been assigned to teach a regular education social studies class. I feel that the only reason I have been given this assignment is because it is an attempt to place me in my licensed area (was the U rating in my special education class of — invalid because it was outside my appointed license) even though I have to go out of my room to teach it and the logistics are proving to be a detriment to adequate instruction at the expense of the students education. I still have no textbooks; I have already been reprimanded in writing for cross teaching subject material and have already received an unsatisfactory formal observation. Also, there is a pattern of cancelled and rescheduled meetings that is disruptive and insidiously unprofessional in its nature and conduct by this administration.

I feel the evidence is justifiable and warrants an overturning of the U rating I received so that I might apply for transfer to another school where my talents might be more appreciated and where my departure is what Mr. ———— desires.

When the principal walked out of the hearing room, his face was chalky white. He slammed the door and stormed down the hallway in an absolute rage. I knew that I had won that hearing. He did too. It was a massacre. I had done my research and had provided a logical and irrefutable case of a concerted effort to manufacture evidence against me because of a personal difference of opinion. I had supplied witness corroboration, references, and documentation. My union counsel who had been assigned to accompany me to the hearing said that in his many years as a counsel he had never seen a case that was so well prepared. He assured me that a verdict was practically guaranteed to come down in my favor.

I was buoyed by the prospect that I was finally going to escape the clutches of this demon. For the next week, whenever I saw the principal in the hallway, he looked dejected and whenever he saw me, he snarled.

At the end of the week, he called me to his office. I was expecting that we would negotiate the terms of my release. He didn't say a word, but I could sense his demeanor had changed. He thrust a letter in my face. He had received the verdict from the hearing first (I got my letter the next day). The ruling had been granted in his favor. I was stunned. I believe he was as well. It was a rigged system. It was as corrupt as anything that a liberal run system could devise, and it had me in its clutches and was not about to let me go. I was trapped like a rat by a cat.

Miracle Escape

After the verdict from the NYCDOE, my days in New York were numbered. I had decided on a personal basis that my time in New York had run its course. This ruling confirmed that it was time to look elsewhere professionally as well. I began applying to positions in New Hampshire. It was time to go home.

However, I ran into the same problems as I did when I was applying to schools in New York. This principal was sabotaging my applications to prospective employers by supplying them with negative information about me. It was a very frustrating and stressful time in my life. My prospects looked bleak.

If I stayed in New York, my future included a lot of time spent in the "rubber room" something that I vowed I would not let happen. Eventually it would lead to termination anyway. I was not going to be held at the discretion of these evil and vindictive people. This was a vice-principal who had failed his certifications multiple times and yet had veto power over my lesson plans because he had not heard of some of the material, even though it was based on verified sources and expert documentation. This was a vice-principal who couldn't even teach a class even though it was rigged to provide the most optimal conditions. And he had lesson material approval over me. His position and authority existed solely at the principal's discretion and his ability to carry out the directives of the principal whatever they might be and never questioning an order. He was nothing but a lackey for the white plantation owner and I had never had an ounce of respect for him.

If I stayed in New York, I was also going to be under the thumb of a man who I considered to be truly evil. This was a man who never cared about kids but only his own personal advancement. He manipulated state testing scores to get false achievement ratings for his school and monetary rewards for himself. Not only unethical but illegal. This was a principal who threw chairs in classrooms, punched walls(once broke his hand punching a concrete block wall) yelled and screamed to get students attention.

He gave me the impression that he despised these kids and was above this assignment in an inner city school. When he came into a classroom it was like he had white gloves on and he did not want to get too close or touch anything that the peasants might have contaminated. He acted like we all had a disease that he did not want to catch. The kids sensed this and they had no respect for him either. Usually when a principal walks into a classroom there is a noticeable change in behavior on the part of the kids. They try to act on their best behavior. When he entered a room there was no perceptible behavior difference. They didn't care about him because he demonstrated that he didn't care about them.

One time we were at an outing and one of the students fell and hit his head on the sidewalk. It appeared serious because the student was unconscious and had fluid leaking from his head. All of us teachers were very concerned and we called the principal over. He barely looked at the student and told us that he was going to get an ice cream and if the student hadn't recovered by the time he came back he would decide then what to do. We decided not to wait. As soon as he left we called 911 and had an ambulance come. It turned out that the student had suffered serious brain trauma and our principal had washed his hands of it.

This was a man who lied and fabricated situations to get his way. He was vindictive and would stop at nothing to ruin the career of anyone who crossed him. This was a man who embodied evil and I refused to be subject to the whims of these kinds of people.

All summer I had applied to various openings in New Hampshire without luck. The summer was quickly coming to an end and I had not secured a teaching position. I was getting ready to go back to New York and face the inevitable with an enormous sense of dread. It was one day before school opened in New Hampshire, New York opened the following week. I had put my fate in God's hands. I did not want to go back to New York but maybe there was a reason. Then I saw a job posting in a school in the White Mountains of New Hampshire. I decided to deliver my resume in person. It was a two-hour ride from my home. When I entered the office, I could see they were in bustling mode the kind that is common in schools around the country that are preparing to start another school year.

I spoke to the secretary, and she directed me into the special education department. I was interviewed within minutes as if they were expecting me. I don't know how that was possible because I had never been there before in my life. The woman in charge of my interview dialed my school in New York to check my references. Naturally I expected the principal to answer, and my interview would be terminated. Turns out the principal was not in the building that day, so the interviewer asked for the next persons on my reference list, who happened to be the head of the special education and the head of the history department. Both gave glowing reviews of my work. I was offered the job on the spot. Fate had intervened in my behalf. It was pure luck that the principal had not been there that day, or my interview would have been torpedoed and it would never have gotten to my references. A couple days later I made one of the most satisfying calls of my life when I called my former school in New York and informed my former principal to his face that I would not be returning for the coming school year, and he could take his "rubber room" and shove it up his ————.

I was ecstatic to say the least. I had escaped from the belly of the beast. I was free, free at last. I would later find out that my liberation was due to divine intervention. The job that I had driven all the way up north for had been filled. But there was another last-minute opening in that school's special education department that they had not yet advertised for. Apparently, they had been expecting a referral to come in and interview for the job. That's why I kept getting the feeling that the whole time that I was being interviewed that I was somehow expected. They mistook me for the referral. I guess the person that they were expecting was a no show. So, in essence it was a case of mistaken identity that allowed me to affect my escape from New York. Call it coincidence if you like, but in my mind, it was nothing short of a miracle.

It was not a perfect job by any means, but it was my steppingstone back to New Hampshire or so I thought at the time. It was a two-hour commute to my home in the southern part of the state. That was not going to be feasible 5 days a week. I would have to find a place to stay during the week. The problem was that New Hampshire paid far less than I had been earning in New York. In fact, I would be making less than half my previous salary—a huge cut in pay. It was true the living expenses were lower in New Hampshire, but I still had to pay my mortgage on my primary residence and that did not leave a lot for renting an apartment as I had done all those years in New York. I would just have to scrimp and watch expenses.

Anything was worth the opportunity I had been given to get out of the clutches of the NYCDOE. Or so I thought. Turns out the arms of the NYCDOE reached all the way into New Hampshire.

I commuted daily for a while until I was able to find a place to rent. Money was tight and I had to pick up any additional work that I could just to make ends meet. I taught Ged courses as well as community college for any stipends that I could pick up. I did this for three years and at the end of that time I was offered tenure by this school. That could have been the end of my association with the education system in New York. I would like to say that my story had a happy ending and that I accepted New Hampshire's offer of tenure and finished out my career there. But that's not what happened.

Because of the length of the commute, I was forced to find employment closer to my residence. That put me back in the job market and back into the jurisdiction of the NYCDOE and my vindictive principal. They continued to send out derogatory information about me whenever I applied for a job and employment verification was requested. I don't know if he ever had the satisfaction of knowing what was happening to me other than there were these requests for employment verification. I know that if he had known it would have sated his vindictive nature to some degree. But I suspect (because of what I heard from other teachers describing his demeanor after I left and that fact that he never spoke about me to anyone) that in his mind I was the one that got away. Over the next several years the best I could get was temporary work filling in for a teacher who had taken leave for a year. I never worked more than one year in one place. I was never again given the opportunity to earn tenure.

I did whatever was required. I did remedial classes, I taught varying grade levels from middle school to high school. I even ran an afterschool program one year. Anything that I could to stay employed. One year, having not yet secured a position for the fall, I was told by a principal that all he could offer me was a job as a paraprofessional (an hourly paid assistant to a regular teacher), but in the end they declined to even do that stating that I was overqualified. I had hit rock bottom.

I had a doctorate and more than a decade of teaching experience and I was unable to land a job as a teacher's assistant. Not even a salaried position. It was then that I realized that cancel culture had won the battle in my professional life. But the evil behind it, the evil that I had encountered in New York and embodied by my principal had not won the war in my personal life. And it never would.

I accepted a position with a non-profit organization that worked with people with mental disabilities. These were people whose mental disabilities were not just learning disorders but impacted their life skills. I became an educator and a counsellor for this organization and this position allowed me to utilize all my skills as a teacher and special education specialist and psychologist without all the rigid constraints of a department of education, a school district and an anal principal breathing down one's neck. It allowed me the creative freedom that I had always aspired to achieve under an oppressive, regressive, authoritarian system. It allowed me the opportunity to do what I always wanted to do and what I did best— help people learn.

For me going into teaching was never about money. I took a huge pay cut when I left the world of high tech and entered the teaching field and now, I was taking another huge cut to work in the world of non-profits. I was looking for a purpose for my life. I thank God every day that I was given the opportunity to work in the education field and be able to help others. I don't think that there is a more gratifying feeling than to be in a profession that serves others. I believe in my heart that it's a Higher calling.

When I was in this part of my career it would have been easy to think that I was above this kind of work and I used to refer to a mantra,

"Teach me to serve humbly in the presence of your creation."

As needy as my students were in New York, the mentally disabled population in New Hampshire required my skills far more. And because of that I was able to have a far greater impact on their lives. And I was doing what I loved. I had found a purpose to my life.

I ended up finishing my career here and retiring and sharing my life with a wonderful woman on (what I consider to be) the cleanest most beautiful lake in the state of New Hampshire—almost a sacred place.

I am back home. My life is serene. I feel that God has truly blessed my life.

For the first time since I can remember my hand does not shake.

I am at peace.

The Crucifixion: The Ugly The Story of DB

Unfortunately this book was always destined to end on a sad note because the ruthlessness of the left and the cancel culture knows no bounds and that includes the destruction of any particular individual who gets in their way. I was just one of many who suffered that fate. You've heard my story. The following story is also true as was everything that proceeded this chapter and the subject of this story was my friend and colleague DB. I tell this to you as my personal dedication to him.

DB and I had a bond right from the beginning. You could say that we were kindred spirits although I would never go as far as to characterize us as soul brothers. That being said there were a lot of parallels in our lives. DB and I were hired at the same time. We were both career changers and were at somewhat similar places in our lives when it came to our ages, raising families and experiencing life in general.

We had both decided to get into education because we wanted to see if we could play a role in helping some less fortunate kids navigate their way through a tough learning environment. I don't think either one of us realistically thought we were going to save the world but we just wanted to be a guide and perhaps be a role model. We both had extraordinary successes and had the rug pulled from under our feet at the height of those successes. We were both opinionated and sometimes found it difficult to keep those opinions to ourselves. It was this trait that got us both into trouble.

At that point we might have been considered A Tale of Two Teachers. I was a conservative. I had learned to be a little better at reining in my opinions. He was an avowed dyed-in-the-wool democrat. He was able to express his opinions unbridled and he did. That was one of the things I liked about him. I always had the feeling that his straight forwardness might be his undoing one day even in the liberal environment of education.

Our political affiliations might have signaled the end of our friendship as it often does today but back then politics did not color every aspect of society. Back then one could abstain from talking about politics and still find plenty of other subjects to talk about and even find common ground because they weren't drenched with political connotations. And we did find plenty to converse about. Our rooms were right across the hall from each other and we usually saw each other at every class change. Often it provided us with an opportunity to chat. Probably the thing that bonded us the most was that we were both history buffs and we were both mentors in the Teaching America's History program.

In a strictly academic sense this program was the thing that I missed most from my New York experience. It was a program that exposed us teachers to materials and methods in order for us to enrich the learning environments of our students. But it was so much more. It was like a history class with the city of New York as its classroom. As a part of this program we got to experience the history of New York like it was a guided tour field trip. We got to engage in passionate and informed discussions with like interested cohorts throughout the city.

We also got to listen to world class instructors, authors, and historians in person. For a student of history it was a learning utopia. It was almost criminal that we were paid for our time as I would have enrolled for free. In fact we should have been paying them for the privilege of taking the course. It taught us inventive ways to be creative with the subject of history and to present it in innovative ways to our students. It unleashed us to think out of the box and we reveled in the experience.

DB and I often shared rides to the conferences and worked on many projects together. DB had special computer skills and also contributed to the class by posting various sources of information that he had researched on any particular topic that the group was engaged in. This drew the attention and praise of the directors in charge of the program. That was DB in a nutshell. Going beyond his own personal needs to help out others. It was an admirable trait for anyone to have, not just for a teacher and it would lead him to great heights but in the end, it couldn't save him from the fate that the left had in store for him.

On paper DB was everything that you would want for a teacher to be successful. He seemed to have the necessary skills, knowledge and credentials to be an effective educator. He was a hard worker and adaptive and a quick learner in regards to the technology that was evolving in the classroom. If some new piece of technology was being introduced to our classrooms (such as a smartboard) he was usually the first to be proficient with it and would often mentor his colleagues on its use. He was known and liked by the rest of the staff.

His one flaw as a teacher was that he was unable to manage a classroom of students. And this was a flaw that was fatal for a career in teaching. Don't get me wrong. None of us teachers had complete control of this population of students but most of us found ways to preserve a somewhat reasonable learning environment. Try as he might and I know he tried everything that he could, he just didn't have the same rapport with students that he had with adults.

A perfect example was the time that he had brought a whole slew of potted plants from his home to the class to illustrate some lesson he was trying to teach. I remember coming into his classroom at the end of the day and he had his head down on his desk and he was sobbing. I was in shock. There was dirt and leaves and shards of pottery all around the room. It looked like a bomb had exploded. The kids had smashed all his potted plants right in front of him. Another time he had tried to borrow a page out of my class and had acquired an ant farm. After only a day that too had been smashed on the floor and all the ants had been squashed.

There were many times that I tried to help him out. If I had a spare period and he had a class I would stay in his classroom and help him with class discipline. But it never translated to him. The kids would behave for me while I was there but as soon as I left they would act up. That's the thing about enforcing discipline, it has its own individual identity. In that sense it is like a personality. It is not easily transferable. It is also hard to change. Once you get branded as soft it is hard to get rid of that label. And the label often gets transmitted from one class to the next, from one year to the next. Very rarely do you get a clean start or a second chance unless you change schools. But DB was an exception to that rule.

He somehow hung onto his job by the skin of his teeth for a couple of years. Our school acquired a new principal in our second year and that probably bought him a bit of a reprieve initially as the new principal got to know his staff. Another year or two in and it was evident even to the new principal, that DB was not going to make it in his present situation.

It was about this time that DB was given a chance to run the computer science class. He accepted with the thought that this new position might not require as much disciplinary skills considering that the kids liked to be on computers and this was a class where they would spend most of their time. DB indicated to me that he was excited to given an opportunity in his area of expertise and we both agreed that it might be a chance to save his career. I could see that he was trying everything that he could to hang in there because despite his tribulations, he had genuinely fallen in love with working with kids and helping them out.

In the beginning it did seem like it was a step in the right direction and might actually work out. However although the students enjoyed the chance to play with computers once the novelty wore off the teacher had the responsibility to protect some expensive equipment. As it turns out I guess there were a couple of instances where some extensive damage occurred on the order of the potted plants and the future of DB was once again in jeopardy.

By this time I had been given tenure by this new principal but I had also had my falling out with him and he was looking to end my career as well. I think it was at this point that my friend DB cut a deal with the devil in order to save his career in education. This principal had recognized the computer skills of DB but was also aware of his deficiencies when it came to controlling a classroom. He had been trying for years to get rid of the librarian who was an older woman.

The principal felt that this kindly old woman who had run the library for 40 years was a relic of the past and was holding back progress. It was true that the woman still ran the library on the Dewey Decimal system but no one knew this library better than her or was more competent. And besides the kids loved her. Her husband had died some years ago and her job at the school was what she lived for. A boss with compassion would have realized that her years of service and dedication had earned her the right to retire when she chose.

But in the eyes of this principal, she was in his way and if she would not leave of her own volition, he would have to push her out. He began to interfere with her duties and harass her so that she would quit. Can you imagine the morals of such a person that feels as if he is justified in intimidating a frail, 70-year-old woman just to get his way? She confided in me many times because I think most of the staff saw me as the point man in the battle against this principal. She was hanging on but only by her fingernails. This behavior on the part of the principal was despicable in my opinion and further convinced me that this man was truly evil. The cruelty of the cancel culture knows no bounds. God help you if you find yourself in their crosshairs.

This is when I believe he conjured up his Faustian agreement with DB. The principal promised DB the librarian's job if he would essentially become a spy for the principal. Just simple things like keeping his ears open in getting intel on his adversaries. For DB, this was a career saver. He would not have to be responsible for teaching classes and managing classroom behavior—but just run the library. A library that would be updated to operate on the latest technology. Right up his alley. The temptation to turn informant would have been irresistible. For DB it was a no-brainer.

He had 5 or 6 years invested in the system and he was making good money. This would preserve that with even more opportunities for pay increases and would provide him with the job security that he had been denied up until now. But to this day I firmly believe that it was not his personal gain that was the foremost reason that he entered into this bargain. I had witnessed him over the years develop a profound love of a job that allowed him to help others especially his kids in a learning setting and he would do almost anything to remain in it.

Knowing the man as I did, I am convinced that it was that love of teaching that motivated his desperation more than anything else. I also believe that the reason that he had difficulty discipling his students was that he was just too kind for his own good. He had a very gentle soul. The kids sniffed it out and took advantage of it. And yet he still didn't hold it against them. Looking back I can't ever remember a time when I saw him angry. Even that day when they destroyed all his personal plants his primary emotion was not one of anger but of sadness. That was DB in a nutshell. If something didn't work out in the classroom he never blamed his students but felt it was something on his end that he could improve. That too was DB.

I've always felt that teaching effectively was like walking on a tightrope and required a delicate balance of enthusiasm, skill, caring and discipline. As long as a teacher came from a place of caring he/she could impose the necessary discipline and still not lose the students. In fact it was the opposite because you gained their respect. And if they respected you, it was more than likely that they would behave better and in turn you would not have to be as militant. It seems to be a simple concept and yet I saw so many teachers struggle to achieve this balance with their students. Earlier I cited a particular case with a Japanese teacher that illustrates this perfectly.

Of course, I or no one else knew it at the time that the usually helpful DB had turned informant. He was still helpful and that was the tool that gained him access to my confidence as well as my colleagues. Suddenly in my case the principal seemed to have knowledge of things that had occurred regarding my classroom that he should not have been privy to. I was getting in trouble for things that no one should have knowledge of.

I started to figure out that the only one I had related some of this information to was DB because I had trusted him. Some of the other teachers began to suspect the same thing. With a little collaboration it didn't take us long to figure out that we had a mole amongst us and who it was. DB quickly became a persona non grata among many of the staff. No one said it to his face but when he was around everyone clammed up especially if there was something confidential or incriminating to be said. That DB was working undercover became the worst kept secret in the school.

I was deeply disappointed in my friend and for a long time I could not understand why he had betrayed our friendship. I had done everything that I could to help him become successful and I was an admirer of his skills and expertise. It didn't take very long to figure out why he had done it. It was only a short period of time later that the woman librarian had announced her retirement (she had finally succumbed to the constant harassment from the principle) and DB was immediately named her successor. Now it all made sense. DB had sold his soul to the devil.

It seemed like things were finally looking up for DB. His job as librarian seemed to be the perfect fit for him and he excelled at it. He totally modernized the library systems and brought it into the twentieth century. Even the part of playing the principal's stooge. By this time I had learned to keep my distance from him as had many others. We still spoke but our conversations were strictly superficial and never of a personal nature.

I had other things on my mind. I had lost my case with the department of education and was staring down the barrel of a rubber room assignment. It was inevitable and only a matter of time, especially if I remained in my current situation. I was desperate to find a way out but I never felt so powerless and so trapped. It was only by a miracle and the grace of God that I was able to effect my escape from this dilemma and make my way back to New Hampshire. I thought I had escaped. The New York portion of my adventure was over but the repercussions would continue to follow me.

I continued to stay in touch with DB over the next few years. Maybe it was the fact that I understood better than most his motivations for becoming a mole and deep down I guess I never truly held it against him. However I'm not sure I completely forgave him either; I just chose to move on with my own life. By this time, he had completely reformed the systems in the library to the principal's satisfaction and the principal was quite impressed with his work. I had heard from some other colleagues as well and DB had continued in his role as snitch. By this time the principal had pretty much cleaned house of any dissenting voices and his power was almost absolute. If you wanted to keep your job under this regime you had better be in total agreement with the agenda.

DB was rewarded for his work and his loyalty. The principal had DB enroll in a training program in order to get his librarian certification and officially become the school librarian at the expense of the school. He was even granted a leave of absence to complete his studies. Graduation was accompanied by tenure and a substantial pay raise and at this point in his career DB was surely making a 6 figure salary. Pretty good for a guy who did not look like he was going to make it out of his second year of teaching. In contrast I was struggling to stay employed.

Things would only get better for DB. He built the same kind of network in the librarian circles that he had built with the Teaching America's History program. He was well known among the city's other librarians and was an excellent source of information. It would be an understatement to say the he was thriving.

Two years later and he was voted The NYCDOE's librarian of the year and presented with his award at a prestigious black tie ceremony. He was the toast of the school district, the city and on top of the world. It was a mercurial ascension to the heights of his profession but even as I congratulated him on his success, I always had a feeling that he had built it on a sandy foundation and that the last chapter was still to be written.

I knew first-hand that the devil is a treacherous bedfellow and cancel culture is ever vigilant and thin skinned. DB had never acknowledged his principal in his acceptance of his award. This was conspicuous by its absence and rather strange since it was this principal who had engineered the library position for DB. I believe that something was afoot.

DB had been in a round table discussion on a DOE policy with some librarians from other schools. DB's principal had been in favor of the policy and DB had posted on this website that he was on the other side of the issue. It was a public post and the principal was made aware of it. It was right there in black and white that DB had publicly countermanded a position that his principal supported. It was in the eyes of the principal a humiliation of unforgivable consequences.

Although I don't know for certain; I suspect that this policy difference was related to testing or evaluation procedures. DB hated standardized testing. He was not a conventional learner. He was imaginative and innovative but put him in a box and he felt stifled. He had dropped out of a couple of schools on his way to becoming a teacher and it was no accident that he became a special education teacher. He empathized with their struggle to succeed in a world of standard testing. He had found ways to overcome and he felt that he could assist special needs students in this area.

In some of his posts around this time he was railing against standardized testing. It was also at this time that his duties as librarian required him to administer and score state and city testing. I have a story to relate about something that happened to us earlier in our careers. We were both fairly new teachers and we had volunteered to grade the state exams for our school along with other teachers from our school.

It was around this time that the Dept of Education in its infinite wisdom had decided to go to a different school evaluation procedure based on a letter system. An 'A' was excellent, and an "F' was designated as a failing school. If a school improved from a lower letter designation to a higher level, there was a substantial monetary bonus to the principal of that school. During that grading session, the teachers were told give full credit to our students on a number of questions that had been deemed ambiguous. Deemed ambiguous by who? The instructions to give full credit had been passed down by the principal.

This seemed to be manipulation of an unethical nature. I remember DB and I looking at each other questioningly. But what did we know? We were just newbies. We followed orders. However, these actions had a dramatic increase in the scores of our students. In the end it resulted in a higher letter grade designation for our school, and it qualified our principal for a bonus. Both of us never forgot that incident and we both remained highly suspicious of the consequences. We both wondered if we had been recruited to do those corrections because we were so new to the teaching game and were less likely to question procedures that did not seem to be above board. I always wonder if this incident had something to do with DB crossing the line with the principal.

I suspect that his falling out had something to do with these testing procedures in one form or another.

For DB, I don't think it was a deliberate insurrection to the authority of the principal. I don't think he meant it as a naked challenge. After all he was part of the regime and he knew how it worked as well as anyone. One can only wonder how many careers had he contributed to their demise in exchange for resurrecting his own. I think it was DB perhaps basking in the light of his newfound status and glory that he felt had earned the right to express an honest opinion. And that his opinion should be valued and taken into consideration. That's all anybody really asks for when they submit their view.

Nevertheless that was all it took. DB's descent was almost as rapid as his rise had been. Everyone who heard about it was bowled over but probably no one was as stunned as DB himself. It was a mere two years before DB went from the apex of his life to the final word in the final chapter. And it shocked all of us who knew about it.

The next 27 months of his life must have been a nightmare beyond anyone's comprehension. For DB, it started out as being frozen out from the principal's inner circle and delegation of some of his responsibilities to other people. The playbook of the left cancel culture is almost always the same. They begin to isolate you then they take away some of your preferences in order to punish you. Then they begin the surveillance, the harassment and intimidation.

DB was eventually demoted and no longer retained his job as librarian although he remained as a teacher within the school. This was the death knell for DB, even if he did have tenure. Tenure meant nothing to this principal. There were ways to get around tenure and no one knew that better than this principal. And of course, his victims. He had perfected the process. Don't forget that it was the principal who knew DB's Achilles heel as a teacher—he struggled with class management. There was no doubt the devil was going to exploit this to achieve his end. And he did.

It wasn't long before DB was being written up on a regular basis for his deficiencies in the classroom. Although he still was protected by his tenure and couldn't be fired for this; he could be rubber roomed. By now the "rubber room" had changed into administrative duties. You were relegated to making copies and other sorts of menial office duties far below the dignity of being a teacher. It was designed to humiliate you and tear down your self-esteem.

In some cases, it would result in a teacher resigning which was an added bonus for the DOE and the principal. The principal would finally be rid of an undesirable and the system would not have to pay a full teacher's salary to someone who was just doing paperwork. A win for everybody but the teacher. Resignation was not an option for DB as he had a family to support. He swallowed his pride and demeaned himself for that paycheck.

After having served a few months in penance he would be returned to his school. At this point he had no real value to this particular school and he was not in the future plans of the principal. He offered to look for another job at another school and there were certainly other schools that would gladly employ him especially with his experience and credentials as a librarian, if not as a teacher. But he would need the reference of the principal. Without that he was trapped in a bleak nowhere land. Where have we heard this before? A change of scenery was not enough to sate this devil and the cancel culture that he was born of and that he spawned. Insolence to this regime required nothing less than total destruction.

Eventually DB would be excessed, another tool in the principal's arsenal. Another step in the process. He still could not be terminated. But without a specific designation within a school, a teacher could be sent into what is effectively the DOE's employee pool. He would still be an employee of the Department of Education but now he could be assigned to wherever they needed him to fill a shortage. If he was lucky, he might end up in a longer-term assignment that offered some stability.

But most teachers were just fill ins for teachers who had called out sick for the day. That meant that you were just a substitute teacher and you had to travel to a different school within the city. I don't have to tell you how difficult this would be for any teacher. I'm sure we all remember how difficult we as students made life for a substitute teacher especially one who was just there for the day. It was the ultimate lame duck situation and elicited the worst behavior from the students. And you had to endure this day after day. A new school, a new class, no real power, the worst behavior. Difficult for any teacher.

It was designed to get rid of the flotsam and the jetsam in the system. Very few survived this designation for very long no matter how much money they were making. I actually saw teachers who would come to the class with a bag of watches and would promise to give every student in the class a watch if they would just behave for that one period. A very expensive proposition-not one that everyone but the well compensated and very desperate could afford to make.

For DB, whose worst nightmare was classroom discipline it was a death sentence, and the principal knew that it would eventually come to this. He could have let him apply to another school and DB would be out of the principal's jurisdiction, but he was bent on DB's destruction and nothing less.

Some people might have said that DB got what he deserved. I was not one of those people. Whatever DB was or had done this was a fate no one deserved. The only lesson to be gleaned was this is what can happen when you cross the cancel culture.

DB to his credit, gamely accepted his fate and tried to make the best of it. He didn't have much choice. I remember some of his posts from this period and although he was trying to accentuate anything that was positive you couldn't help but feel that there was a profound sense of depression, sadness, and desperation behind his words. He was in a downward spiral despite the happy face he tried to show the world.

From here the descent into the whirlpool was swift. I wasn't privy to it all, but I understand there were accusations of theft and inappropriate behavior on DB's part. This was an actionable offense. It is not clear whether Dave was fired, or he quit to avoid his dismissal but, in any event, he separated from the Department of Education.

I know his spirit was crushed at this point because he knew that he was finished forever in the field of education something that he had finally found his niche in. Something that he had learned to love. It was the cruelest trick they could have played on him. He had struggled and worked so hard to stay in the system and they had dangled the ultimate prize in front of him and then they had it snatched from him in the blink of an eye.

I know he was completely devastated by this turn of events. That's all the leftist cancel culture really wants. They want to crush your will to resist and demand complete submission to their authority. Once they have achieved that end and hollowed you out as a person they don't care all that much what happens to the husk that remains.

Some of his posts from this time were extremely sad and we all offered him our wishes of support and hope and encouragement. I think that he was crushed by it all. He soon had some domestic problems. He had an accident and suffered a serious neck injury. He was incurring financial difficulties. Mentally he seemed be aloof and erratic. All this terminated in the breakup of his marriage and family.

He was asked to leave his home. The spiral only continued. He was living in an apartment in the city but soon became homeless. I will let some of his social media posts from this time in his life tell his story in his own words.

"I need some positive thoughts to help me through some very hard times. I have hit a new low."

"I have been railroaded". He says he knows who engineered it but won't disclose it publicly.

"I am essentially a house substitute teacher for a week at each school."

"ATR is basically assigned to senior staff that the DOE wants to get rid of."

"Spent the last two periods with an 8th grade special education class. I am clearly out of mental and emotional shape for dealing with these kids."

"Shoot me now. I have just spent 4 days co-teaching in an inclusion kindergarten. I have gone home thoroughly exhausted each day. The only thing that kept me from completely losing it today was the knowledge that tomorrow-Friday-would be my last day in the class and Monday I would start a different adventure in a different school. Not so fast. I came home and looked at my work email (you'd think I'd be able to do that at work wouldn't you) only to find out I was assigned to the same school and most likely the same class."

"Spent Thanksgiving at the Bowery Mission. They put out 1800 full blast turkey dinners in one day for needy New Yorkers. Great people, volunteers and staff. Make everyone feel truly welcome. Everyone also gets a brand new winter coat, grooming supplies and other necessities. What a wonderful way to start the day." The responses he got to this post were of the nature that it is such a great feeling to help out needy people isn't it. All his friends assumed that he was a volunteer worker in this venue. Later they were all shocked to discover that by this time he was no longer employed and for all intents and purposes, homeless. He was not a volunteer at this food kitchen, he was a recipient.

Not long after this, his posts stopped, and he went dark. Without a job and without a home, he took to the streets. He was living in a homeless shelter when a mentally disturbed inmate broke into his living space one night and nearly decapitated him with a knife. From the time that he was on stage to accept his award for being voted librarian of the year until they wheeled him out of a homeless shelter on a coroner's gurney and took his body to the morgue spanned 27 months. Despite everything he had done for his school and more importantly the students and everything that he had achieved—he was deemed expendable. In the eyes of the cancel culture everyone is. He was just another cog in the machine that had to be stripped out when it malfunctioned. No one is irreplaceable. No one escapes cancel culture. I thought that I did but I found that this culture has long tentacles. Dave didn't escape either. He found out that cancel culture retribution trumps all. Cancellation is king.

And as far as I am concerned this principal, this system that spawned him and the cancel culture that he represents has DB's blood all over their hands. This one man was the embodiment of woke-ism and cancel culture. Calculating, manipulative, dishonest, amoral, cold, ruthless, heartless evil. This did not have to happen this way. Come to your own conclusion. Call it what you want. I was there for most of it and I am convinced that this was nothing less than a crucifixion. By a culture that knows no bounds. I was fortunate enough to escape paying the ultimate price on the altar of woke-ism. I was the one that got away. I shudder to think that my colleague DB was the sacrificial lamb in my place.

There by the grace of God go I.

THE BIG PICTURE

Disclaimer: Dear reader; please be advised that you enter this phase of the book at your own risk. Any resemblance to tactics and schemes presently employed by leftists, liberals and democrats is not purely a coincidence—it is intentional.

"If you tell a lie big enough and keep repeating it, people will eventually come to believe it."

Joseph Goebbels

When Hitler and the Nazis took over Germany in 1932, they recognized that in order to solidify their power it was vital that they control crucial elements of society. One of the elements was the media and another was education. It was what the Nazi's referred to as "synchronization". There is a great parallel to what is happening in America today. It is a pattern of operation that we will see played out over and over again. It is almost as if the left has stolen the playbook of Nazi Germany and employed it for their purposes and yet they are the ones who resort to calling President Trump, a Nazi.

The strategy of the left and the Nazis was similar in that they were both designed to control the population in order to perpetuate their power. Control of the majority equals power. I submit that the left has perfected this manipulation by masterfully coordinating the two elements, so they dovetail together like hand in glove. The difference is that the Nazis were nationals who wanted to restore Germany to international prominence. The left wants to use their power to reduce America's presence on the world stage and we will get into this matter in more detail, in another chapter. But as proof of this, one only has to look no further than Barack Obama and his apology tour, just after he was elected when he went around the world apologizing for the evil that America had inflicted on all the other countries of the world.

However, before the left began employing these techniques, there were the Nazis and they were some of the most evil architects the world has ever known.

State of Education in Nazi Germany

The Nazis were quick to recognize that the schools held the future of Germany. Moreover, they were the future of his ideology and so Hitler viewed them as the training grounds and recruitment centers for his purposes. He knew that he was going to need an army and they were his future soldiers. The purpose of the schools in the Hitlerian scheme of things was to indoctrinate students into the racial ideas of the Nazi party and to extract a personal allegiance to the Fuhrer. Aryan mothers were conditioned to further the pure Aryan race and prepare their sons to be loyal soldiers.

The tools of purge and replace were the first steps in the takeover of the education system. All Jewish teachers were fired. A Nazi teachers association was created in order to screen teachers for their racial and political compatibilities. A teacher was required to become a member and compliance was close to 100%.

Teachers were trained in the Nazi ideology. If they did not teach the Nazi ideology in an effective manner in the classroom, the pupils could report their teachers to the authorities. Now there's a novel concept. If the teachers in our current system could be put on report for being ineffective educators, we would have a lot of empty classrooms.

There was an incident of a German teacher who grew weary of the regimentation that was imposed on the learning process. He implored his students to just have a conversation with him, like normal human beings and not like "programmed robots and automatons". He was reported to the authorities and sent to a concentration camp. My, my, how we have evolved and civilized we have become since then. In America or at least New York City, if a teacher is put on report, they are sent to a Rubber Room. (A kind of detention room for teachers on suspension.)

Textbooks that did not exemplify the Nazi's vison of German greatness, were thrown into huge bonfires and the Nazi controlled press began rewriting the new version of events. That's the protocol. Once you purge, you have to follow up and replace it.

That includes the curriculum. Religious education was banned. That sounds vaguely familiar. Eugenics replaced religion. Physical education was emphasized in place of some of the sciences built on reason and logic. Hitler had enough scientists—what he needed was obedient soldiers. It is eerily similar to what the schools of today are turning out—soldiers for the leftist cause. The German version of the boy scouts at that time was taken over by the Hitler Youth which was essentially a more targeted and accelerated military training program.

The Nazi domination of the education system would ensure obeisance to the Nazi ideals for generations and the result was a soulless, mindless automaton who would be complicit in the murder of six million Jews. It explains how the Holocaust was made possible.

A mindless, soulless, sycophant has similarities to what is occurring in American schools and society today. This is the same blueprint that the leftists are following.

This is where the democrats learned to perfect their strategies.

The State of Education in America

"The philosophy of the schoolroom in one generation is the philosophy of government in the next." (Abraham Lincoln)

"We don't need no education
We don't need no thought control
No dark sarcasm in the classroom
Teachers leave them kids alone
Hey, teachers, leave them kids alone
All in all its just another brick in the wall
All in all you're just another brick in the wall"
'Another Brick in the Wall' song by Pink Floyd

Liberals were smart enough to recognize the importance of exercising control over our youth. The liberal movement in the school system started in the colleges with protesters over the Vietnam War. Student and professors joined in expressing their dissatisfaction with the American government. As radical and left leaning students graduated, they got jobs as professors and teachers and over time they not only infiltrated colleges but the public schools as well. Once they had sufficient control over the key components of the school environment and the school boards, they were able to put in place their campaign to indoctrinate students, according to their liberal values and agendas.

As they graduate more students who also become teachers for the cause, the system perpetuates itself and ultimately conservatives are squeezed out. I found it outrageous that as a conservative educator, I was essentially mandated to join the teacher's union and my dues were used to make campaign contributions to democratic candidates—people I would never vote for in a million years.

Presently all aspects of our schools are dominated by liberals and our country has become the product of that liberal cultivation. Liberals are beginning to reap what they have sowed. That may have been the biggest mistake the conservative movement in this country has made— underestimating the impact of influence in our education system and surrendering it so easily to the liberals. In my opinion we will pay a huge price for this miscalculation as we will see later, because it is fundamentally changing our society and the way it thinks.

One of the hardest parts of writing this book, for me, was having to include the section on the state of our education system in this country. It was as if in the writing of this book I had to relive the crime all over again. I was a frontline witness to the destruction it did to our children. Truth be told, I was more than a witness, I was an unwitting accomplice and it broke my heart almost daily, once I realized what was happening.

You must understand something. There is a realization to be grasped here. And once you recognize that realization, a light will come on and everything will begin to make sense. You will see how all the pieces fit together into one giant puzzle and only then will it all make perfect sense. And it all begins with the education system.

That realization didn't happen for me right away. Call me naïve and I guess that's what I was, but I think I can be forgiven this fault given the circumstances. Before I reveal my epiphany let me take you on a little journey that might explain how I happened on this discovery.

The reason that I got into teaching was that I thought I would be good at getting students to learn. I felt that I had gotten a solid education when I was in grade school and it had served me fairly well throughout my life. I thought that it would be a platform for an effective career as an educator. All of my life I loved to learn about new things and that was fueled by a love of reading. I was fortunate to have been encouraged to read from an early age. In many of my early grades, students were given prizes by the number of books that they read and reviewed, in the course of the school year. I think I would have been an avid reader even if it hadn't been incentivized because I enjoyed it. I also had a model.

My father also supported my reading and was the perfect role model. This from a man who never made it past the sixth grade and yet he could carry an intelligent conversation, on almost any subject with anybody. He was a man who had a veracious appetite for learning.

He was forced to drop out of school to go to work to help his family survive the depression. Then came World War II, where he served as a tail gunner in twenty missions over Europe. Having survived the war, he returned home and could have gone to school on the GI bill but chose to get married and start a family. With a family to support, he forsook a chance at education to work in a steel mill. He spent the rest of his life there and hated almost every minute of it.

But every Saturday (with me in tow when I was younger) he went to the library and checked out at least 10 books to read and finished them all before the next Saturday. And he did that every week of his life. The result was that he was one of the smartest men that I ever knew. And he was adamant that his kids get an education above everything else. (Of course, that was a time long, long ago and far, far away when parents trusted schools to educate their children.)

He was so dedicated to that proposition that after I graduated from high school, I was seriously considering foregoing college (even though I had secured an athletic scholarship) and following in his footsteps as a steel worker. In fact, I started working in the steel mill that summer but when fall came I was mysteriously fired from my job. With few options available I decided to attend college and it was a decision that profoundly transformed my life.

I can promise you with the highest degree of certainty that had I not gone down *that* path, I would not be in any position to be sitting here writing this book. I would not have had the skills, the life experiences or the opportunities required for writing and producing a work of this nature. It wasn't until many years later, that I learned that my father had persuaded the foreman to fire me because he knew in his infinite wisdom, that I would never have been satisfied with his lot in life as a steelworker.

My father passed away before I got my doctorate and even though I know he would have been proud of that accomplishment, I was never as educated as my father, who never got past the 6th grade. It was because he read more than I ever did, and he was self-educated. To this day I have never met anyone who read as much as he did.

But then, I never met Abraham Lincoln. He too was a totally self-educated man.

"All I have learned, I learned from books." Abraham Lincoln

One thing that my father was always grateful for in his limited exposure to education was that it taught him to read. It was the greatest gift it could have ever given him. The ability to read unlocked the whole world and all the knowledge accumulated by man was now available to him. Now he was only limited by what he wanted to learn. It was his ticket to self-educate. It was better than any school-taught degree. And before you can think critically about things you have to be able to read about them. The greatest thing that parents can do for their children is to read to them when they are young and encourage their reading throughout their lives.

Anyway, with my background as a basis, I thought that I would be good at inspiring young students to learn and that's why I became a teacher. Perhaps I was naïve in my idealism. Imagine someone getting into a profession with the idea that maybe they could make other lives better. In teacher speak, everyone repeats the same mantra "They just wanted to make a difference".

A primary goal of the Teach America organization (which lent to my deception) was that they were trying to improve the quality of education by attempting to break the cycle of incompetence. The theory was that undesirable areas or subject matters attract the worst teachers and those teachers turn out less educated students who in turn become teachers in the same underprivileged neighborhoods. Thus, the poor quality of education is perpetuated like a self-fulfilling prophecy.

When I was teaching, I would see evidence of this constantly. Whenever I walked into an English classroom in the school that I was assigned to, I would find the writing on the blackboard (written by the teacher) covered in spelling and grammatical errors. This would have been unimaginable in my grade school classroom as a youth.

The intention of a group like Teach America was to infuse areas identified as deficient, with new blood (usually from outside) that had the necessary skills and qualifications to raise the overall standards of education, in that particular area or school. They did that by offering idealism, incentives and requiring that their recruits commit to a contract of a certain number of years.

It was kind of like the Peace Corps meets enlistment in the armed forces, only with benefits. I must have hit the trifecta on the disadvantaged spectrum—as I was assigned to teach science(a subject nobody wanted to teach anymore) to special education students(a population no one wanted to be associated with) in a minority neighborhood(that looked more like a war zone) in the Bronx, New York(where no one wanted to go).

The first thing I noticed about educators was the metrics of the system. In the private sector employee success was measured by results. In education, employee success is measured by longevity. For every year that you participate in the system, the higher you are paid, which in turn directly drives your retirement. The pay scale is written right into the teacher contract and you know exactly what you will earn in any given year that is covered by the contract.

And that is *regardless* of your performance as a teacher.

In this system, you don't have to be good at your job, you just have to be good at hanging around.

The only time that performance seems to be of any significance is when you are trying to get tenure. Tenure (for those unfamiliar with the system) is kind of like an apprenticeship, in the first few years of a new teacher. In that period of time, if a school or a principal decides that for any reason you are not a good fit, they can terminate you unconditionally.

On the other hand, if they decide that they want to retain you, they will grant you tenure and that is essentially the golden ticket that entitles the teacher to a job for life. After achieving tenure, teacher performance is almost inconsequential to job retention, unless you do something egregious—like sexual misconduct or something of that nature.

The only value that I ever saw in tenure is that it protected teachers, in the event that they worked for a vindictive principal, who just wanted to get rid of teachers because of personal dislike. Principals in New York City are afforded an inordinate amount of power over all aspects of their school, but at least their power was somewhat restricted when it concerned a teacher who had attained tenure. Especially when it concerned a teacher who was a conservative.

Tenure was a good thing when it concerned a good teacher and a bad principal because it afforded that teacher some security, but it worked to the detriment of the students when you have a good principal and a bad teacher. The latter is a lot more common than the former, and it is reflected in the poor state of affairs of the education system and its protectionist union.

Tenure is probably one of the worst concepts in a system that is predicated on seniority. The end result is that it rewards mediocrity and perpetuates incompetence. That and the teacher's unions who perpetrate the complete hoax—that they care about the education of our children—are the worst indictments of our education system.

The only thing the teacher unions care about is remaining in power so that they can control the whole system, even if it is failing our students. If teacher unions really cared about the welfare of our children, they would not be so strenuously opposed to charter schools, when in almost every instance, charter schools are outperforming their public- school counterparts.

In minority school districts parents of black and Hispanic students are on their hands and knees pleading for school choice and are being denied that option by the teacher unions and the political influence they command. Their children are hopelessly trapped in these failing schools and they know it. Is that how the union shows it concern for students?

They have even gone so far as to close down charter schools that had proven successful track records. How good was that for the students who benefitted from being in those schools? Don't be fooled by the teacher unions. They don't care about your kids. And that is your first lesson. That was my first realization. But that is just the beginning.

It gets worse.

A lot worse.

Let me start off by saying, that in my opinion students today are getting the short end of the stick by our public education system. Many of the teachers I witnessed had no skills to be in front of a classroom. They relied solely on the fact that kids were required to be in a classroom until a certain age and therefore the public school system is guaranteed a captive audience.

A perfect example was a science teacher, who I was assigned to assist in an inclusion class. What that meant was that she was assigned a regular education class of say, twenty-five students but also six special education students. However, the six special education students had to be accompanied by a special education teacher, (which was me) to assist them with help they may need, answer questions and support them with any extra guidance that they might require.

I always thought science was one of the best subjects to teach learning challenged students because a teacher could make it interactive and hands-on with the number of experiments you could do. Apparently, this teacher held an entirely different view of teaching science. Her method was to pull out the science textbook (which we were finally supplied) and begin reading word for word from the text. She never took any questions. She barely made eye contact with the students in the class until she was done reading.

Then there were questions in the textbook at the end of each chapter and she would assign these for the students to work on. Every day was the same routine for 90 minutes twice a week. This was her class, she was in charge, I had no say in how it was conducted, and not once did she ask me for any input. I can tell you the students who I was assigned to assist, abhorred every minute of this teacher's instruction and I could not blame them. Even for me as a teacher, this was the most mind-numbing exhibition of learning I had ever witnessed.

There was no element of teaching that I could discern from this method. She just read from the textbook and did not deviate one iota. Why not just assign the chapter for the students to read themselves?

She obviously equated her reading of the chapter verbatim, with the skill of teaching. There were students that would have preferred jumping out of the window, rather than endure another 90-minute session with her. Fortunately, we were on the ground floor so it would not have had the desired effect.

Naturally student behavior in the class escalated and by the end of the year, most of the students had been kicked out of the class. Students who should have been in a classroom that was exposing them to the principals of science, were sitting in detention hall because of a teacher who did not have a clue how to present an engaging lesson. The sad part is that the kids in detention hall, were getting just as good an education as the kids in the science class itself—none.

And yet to my complete and utter astonishment, the administration loved this teacher. She was always right on schedule with the track of her curriculum and her grades and paperwork were always current and delivered on time. At faculty meetings she was always getting praise from the principal and presented as an example for the rest of us to follow. I could not believe *this* was the example that the education system held in high regard. There was no real learning going on in that classroom and the administrators were perfectly fine with that.

I am sure that this teacher had a long and successful career in education and not one of her students ever learned a damn thing in her class. The only way a teacher of this nature could even hold her job, never mind thrive, is because of the teacher unions and the climate in the school systems. Our children are captive audiences in these horrendous learning environments and is it any wonder that they are graduating without any discernible skills?

You better hang onto your hats because they are about to be blown away. It's a foul wind that blows through the hallways of our schools, nowadays.

In contrast, I found myself in a situation that I deemed inexplicable. I was being mentored at the time by an organization called Telling America's Story. I mentioned earlier in this book about "Forgotten Patriots" a story about Revolutionary War prisoners who died on prison ships, rather than swear allegiance to the crown of England.

On this particular day we were studying that book. It had just been released and was hailed by the historical community as cutting-edge material. There were copies of the book available to us educators as well as an instructional DVD. Edwin Burrows, the author, came to speak about his book to our group. It was an impressive presentation. As a result, I worked up a lesson plan on the subject matter based on the materials I had been given.

I was so excited that I was going to be able to deliver such an exciting, ground-breaking lesson to my class. But first I had to have the lesson plan approved by the principal's office. However, since there was no mention of the patriots held as prisoners in the textbook we were using, I was prohibited from delivering the lesson. It was one of the greatest episodes of American patriotism and it was not going to be permitted because it was not in some textbook that was probably ten years old. I was beside myself to say the least. From this experience I learned that the textbook was regarded as the Holy Grail of all instruction. You know the one. The textbook that new teachers don't get issued until the year is almost half over. Yea that's the one.

On some of the cable news shows that I watch, reporters go out into the streets and ask questions of ordinary passers-by. There are all different generations represented in these 'man-in-the-street' interviews but generally the majority of respondents come from the younger generations such as Gen Xers and millennials. They appear to be college graduates in their mid-twenties, now out in the working world.

One of the questions was "Who fought in the Civil War? This is a pretty straight forward question in my opinion and only requires a basic knowledge of American history. Very few got it right. The other answers were embarrassing and ranged from foreign countries to foreign continents.

Another question on Thanksgiving Day was "Who was at the first Thanksgiving." I was stunned at the answers that were given. One person said that he believed "that there were some people from

Sweden." Someone else who was trying to be cute in their attempt to display their obvious expertise on the subject and responded in this manner, "In nineteen hundred and forty-two, Columbus sailed the ocean blue." No, what you just read was not a misprint. This person was beaming proudly as if they had just recited the Gettysburg Address from memory.

In another instance, when the reporter asked the question, the person stated immediately that they had no clue. The reporter tried to help out and actually give a clue and said "It was the Pil...."

When the person in the street heard the first three letters her eyes lit up with that lightbulb that goes on in your head when you think you've just recognized what the answer is. Then just as quickly the light went out and the response was, "I don't have a clue."

What is so sad about this is that these are young adults who are out in the working world and have been in the public-school system for as many as 12 or 13 years. This is what we are graduating. This is our finished product. These are the future leaders of our country.

My question is "What are we doing with those 13 years if we are not even teaching the rudiments of a basic education? Unfortunately, having been in the system for 15 years, I know what the answer is.

Our schools don't care about educating our children.

In fact, the converse is true. If we truly cared about education in this country, we would demand some sort of accountability. When a college graduate cannot identify who was at the first Thanksgiving, every social studies teacher that that student ever had from grade school to college should be summarily fired. It is disgraceful what our schools are turning out. A current study of a comparison of students from other countries found that Asian students are 4 grade levels above American students.

"This is one of the most damning indictments of our education system that I have ever come across, and it is yet another clear indication that what we are doing is simply not working. Our children are not being given the tools that they need to compete in our modern society and we have only ourselves to blame." (End of the American Dream 12/4/2019 by Michael Snyder)

But more on this in the next section.

Having spent 15 years in the education system as a teacher, special education case manager and mental health counsellor, it has always been a theory of mine that the system, even though they claimed to the contrary, never wanted to graduate kids who could think for themselves. In fact, I always believed that the exact opposite was the goal of the people (liberals) in charge of the education system in our country. Now some of you may be shocked at this statement but let me try to explain further by using examples from my career in teaching.

I was a career changer when I got into education. I really regretted that I had not gotten into it sooner, as I really loved it and it always felt that I had found my niche in life. I always said that I loved the job, but I despised the system. I was always guided by the precept that I knew my students were not going to remember all the names and dates that would be covered in the course of a year and that was to be expected. However, if they came away with anything from being in my class, it was the ability to think critically. I did not want to give them a fish, I wanted to teach them how to fish, so they could feed themselves for the rest of their lives. But unfortunately, this runs exceedingly counter to the objectives of the education system. Their prime directive is not to teach students *how* to think but *what* to think.

There are a lot of "bad" teachers in the education system just like the one that was described earlier, who recited her textbook. Most have never been properly trained (and I contend that is by design) others are lazy, and some are just incompetent. The teacher unions perpetrate the whole failing system.

"Government unions have politicized and polarized our teachers-on purpose-by silencing the voices and values of teachers and parents…I learned that damaging undertow my very first month as a student teacher. We can debate, deliberate and assign 'experts' to the issues and rob another fifty years' worth of students of their best hope at success, or we can start listening to the real experts-parents and teachers-and win our schools and country back." (Rebecca Friederichs, "Standing up to Goliath")

As a result, our kids are trapped in this "another brick in the wall" environment. Outside of school, everything around them is telling these students that education has no relevance to their lives. Theirs is a tough life on the streets with poverty, violence, guns, knives, drugs and death. Where does education fit into that scenario? When they do get in the school, the thinking that school has nothing to offer them is only reinforced by an authoritarian environment of boring teachers, using uninspiring methods to promote conformity. And all that is acerbated by mental, emotional, and learning disorders such as ADHD, autism etc. that create a learning space that is volatile at best.

It's an atmosphere where a physical confrontation can result in fists flying and desks being overturned at any time, where cursing is commonplace, where bars on windows is normal and where kids who can't commit suicide by jumping through an upper floor window will resort to throwing themselves down a stairwell instead. It's a place where kids are just as likely to be taken out of school in handcuffs or in a straight- jacket. It is no wonder that kids see school as a place that has nothing to offer them.

The Issue of Poverty

Poverty is in itself its own separate culture. Instances of poverty can be found in what appear to be affluent school districts. It is a common denominator of many school districts and it has its own characteristics and impact on the educational environment. The manifestations of poverty are eerily similar no matter where it is found. It is characterized by broken homes, children raised in the extended family—usually with a matriarchal head, drug abuse and alcoholism, run-ins with the law and a lack of respect for authority and adult. In many instances poverty has become generational and its culture is the legacy that is passed down.

The greatest impact on schools is probably the lack of respect for authority and adults. Children have grown up in an environment where there is not a single adult role model that they respect. Even worse they may have been abused by an adult, which tends to destroy all trust in adults. Many boys are often forced to assume the male responsibilities of the family in the absence of the father. The absence of the patriarchal presence is particularly pronounced in the inner city. Mothers become the authority figures and it makes it especially difficult for students raised in these families to relate to male authority figures. Another factor that compounds the situation is that female teachers often outnumber the male teachers in most school systems and these are the role models that these students desperately need.

Another characteristic of people in poverty that I discovered is that their scope is very limited and immediate. They live in the here and now and they rarely look outside of those boundaries. Their neighborhood is all that concerns them and it is hard to get them to consider that there is a whole world outside of the street they live on. Many of these students are just trying to survive day to day and it is their street skills that are essential to this end, not whether they can do algebraic equations or not. They don't see education as a relevant entity in their struggle to survive and this attitude (which may just be the product of their circumstances) has a devastating undermining impact on the education process in schools.

The other thing that surprised me was that for people who came from such impoverished backgrounds—how much emphasis they put on material possessions. These are people who have difficulty affording food and yet they try to send their kid to school with the best sneakers or the latest electronic gadget because this is what confers status in this culture. And God help the poor kid who comes to school without these trappings. They are ridiculed relentlessly to the point of social pariah. That is why I understand any school that adopts school uniforms in order to eliminate these differences in physical appearances, as much as possible. Any argument against the loss of individual creativity should be measured against the reduction of aggression in these environments. School has always been and probably always will continue to be a cruel place. The social ramifications of injustices committed to children in these circumstances can be devastating to one's esteem-scarring some for the rest of their lives and driving others to commit deadly acts not only to themselves but to the perpetrators around them. Any policy aimed at reduction of aggression should be seriously weighed.

The State of Society in America.

"Do y'all remember, before the internet, that people thought the cause of stupidity was the lack of access to information? Yeah. It wasn't that." (Facebook meme from Crazy World)

"Liberalism is a mental disorder." (Michael Savage)

The education system was always the template. It was always the microcosm for what the left wing wanted to do to the rest of the country. They enlisted a complicit and corrupted news media in an endless assault of mind control on our young unsuspecting citizenry and the result is the creation of yet another bubble.

Today's society is afflicted by the "snowflake bubble". The "snowflake bubble" is filled with air from the over-inflated self-esteem. It too, as we saw with other bubbles, has no foundation in reality. In this case, it has no relevance to earned achievement. It stems from the liberal concept that everyone deserves a trophy. It is a protective cocoon created from an illusion of how wonderful they think life is until they are confronted with adversity and then they melt, hence the term 'snowflake'.

Liberals feel they can say anything to attack conservatives but if they are criticized in the slightest, they cannot handle it. In real life, if you want to dish it out, you better learn to take it. Someone forgot to tell the liberals about that part. They expect it to be only one way—their way. This is why they hate Trump—he fights back and they can't cope with it.

Critical Thinking

You see dear readers; the education system is only incompetent if you look at it from the point of view that you want your child to learn all he/she can and be successful in life. But if the PURPOSE of the education complex is to dumb your child down so they become too dumb to think for themselves too dumb to ask questions and too dumb to do anything but be compliant Then the public school system is anything but incompetent. It is accomplishing what it set out to do.

It reminds me of a quote—"If children remain uneducated then they are too stupid to overthrow the government."

Isn't this what occurred during the time of slavery in this country? The more that slaves were brought into the country the more that the white slave owners became the minority. This enclave of slave owners was so vastly outnumbered that their greatest fear was that there would be an uprising of slaves and the whites would be wiped out. How were such a small number of elite able to control the vast majority? They did it by outlawing the education of slaves and forbidding them to congregate. They kept them in the dark and they kept them from conspiring together and it was largely successful.

The school districts of today are the plantations of the past. In this sense the democrats have been grooming their electorate for 50 years. The news media in this country has been leftist for just about as long but they were only exposed for what they really are since the 2016 election of Donald Trump. Now they are just a publicity propagandist wing of the Democratic party. Any pretense that they are impartial has been destroyed.

The ratings for the mainstream media have been plummeting in the last few years because people recognize the corruption. When they want to get some semblance of actual news or the truth, they know they won't get it from CNN or MSNBC or the mainstream corporate media. Conservatives were the first to abandon their viewership of mainstream media. Independents were the next group to flee. Finally, even some liberals have wandered over to more conservative news outlets like Fox.

The few people who are left that faithfully watch mainstream media are the success stories of the education system. They are the die hard, leftist sheep who would follow the Democratic agenda without question right over a cliff if necessary. They are a special kind of stupid. They don't have an inkling of what critical thinking is.

I have referred to my situation often up to now as a conservative problem. My conservative values were what got me in trouble with the liberal administrators and that is true. They didn't like my politics and they didn't like my views on religion or patriotism or my insubordination. All those were contributing factors. But to get to the core of it what they really didn't like was that I was trying to teach my students critical thinking. That is what really made me an enemy of the state. That is what ran counter intuitive to their agenda and necessitated my cancellation.

With some of my classes, after we had covered the curriculum that was required, I would use our extra time to examine things that they wanted to learn about, rather than what was dictated to us by the school. Some of the things we looked at in our class was the Titanic, mysteries about the pyramids and the Kennedy assassination. I learned a lot about them from the examination of these various topics.

The Kennedy assassination is a perfect example. This was a historical event of major significance. Of course, I realized the high school students that engaged in this study were born some 40 years after this event happened. Very few had ever heard of Kennedy, knew who he was or that he had been assassinated. However, every November there is no shortage of documentaries, movies and theories presented on television revisiting the event. If anyone had any curiosity whatsoever, the information is readily available. And this is where we are with the condition of our education in this society. No one bothers to seek anything out on their own. Oh sure, the class was fascinated by the events once it was presented to them but I was still stunned that they were so oblivious to the subject and no one else had felt that it was important enough to introduce it to them. We spent time viewing some of the documents, reading some of the material and discussing some of the theories.

I love when the topic is controversial as the Kennedy assassination because at the end, I ask them to write down what they think happened and give their evidence to support it. They were not going to be graded on this because there would be no right or wrong, but this was critical thinking in all its glory. They were presented with a situation and a set of facts and they were going to have to analyze it, come out with a premise and provide evidence that supported that premise. This was a skill that would serve them well for the rest of their lives and as a teacher, I was excoriated for teaching it in the classroom.

I have a personal example to relate that illustrates just how powerful the critical thinking experience can be. I was always a big proponent of field trips as opposed to classroom and learning out of a book. I think that anytime you can take a student to see a real object or a real place where history has occurred, you are providing the best possible learning experience. Especially as opposed to relying on a graduate just out of a liberal learning factory that has barely read a textbook on the topic and is programmed to present it at the behest of liberal administrators. If you really care about your child's education and want them to truly become aware and comprehend our history, I would advise that you take them to visit as many actual places as you can.

That is an invaluable experience and one that is likely to remain with them and serve them for a longer period. I recently took a trip around the country and I saw and did so many incredible things that I know I will remember and be able to recount for the rest of my life. It gives you a perspective that you just cannot get out of a book or even watching a film. For examples, one of the places we visited was the last stand battlefield of General George Custer.

Now I have read several books on the subject and studied the accompanying maps, but nothing I had done previously brought it more to life for me than standing on the actual battlefield where that event took place. I was able to view the actual terrain, the geography of the area, the logistics of where the soldiers were as opposed to the Indians, what each saw from their particular perspective, what they might have been thinking. And most important, what caused each proponent to act the way that they did. Finally, I was able to see the actual places where the soldiers fell and their final resting places. I felt like I had walked through a door that allowed me to be an observer to a historical event—something that a book or a movie could never achieve. I was moved in a way that could never happen with a book or a movie.

This is the kind of immersion that inspires real learning and I realized that I wish I could have taken every one of my students on that journey. We would have learned so much together and I am talking about genuine learning that sticks to your mind and it becomes an experience that you carry with you for the rest of your life. That to me is a real educated person. Compare that to all the liberal, leftist, college education system graduates whose knowledge is so shallow they cannot tell you who fought in the Civil War.

For an even more profound effect combine critical thinking with a historical event and a visit to a historical site. This is what an exercise in that kind of analytical thinking might look like.

I remember when John F. Kennedy was killed. It was a cool, overcast Friday in late November and the principal came into my fifth-grade class and said that there was an incident with the President of the United States, and we were going to be dismissed early. He did not actually say JFK was dead although I think that had been reported by then, but I think he felt it was better that we got that news when we got home and were with our families.

That was a time when school did not try to be "the be all and end all" to their students and respected parents' rights and their roles in raising their own children When I got home my mother had the television on and it was all over the news and that is when I learned he was dead. Certainly, at that age I would not have been able to grasp the repercussions and significance of the event, but I felt as if I had lost a friend and I felt like crying.

I was pretty invested in JFK and I remember that I had stayed up late the night of the election just a few years before. Finally, my mother had to send me to bed as there was still no result and I had school the next morning. It was not until I got up to go to school the next morning, that I learned that JFK had won the presidency. He was smart, good looking and had a self-deprecating sense of humor that not only captivated me but the whole country.

Over the next few years, he dominated the news (I especially remember the tense days of the Cuban missile crisis) and I thought he was such a great president. And now he was dead. My mother reassured me that someone else would take over and they would be competent enough to run the country and we would all be fine. I guess that was enough assurance to keep me from crying and I went out to play with my friends. Nevertheless, I could not get rid of the feeling of emptiness that we had lost something, our perception that the world was a safe place, our innocence, something I could not put my finger on or articulate at the time. Something I just felt.

Two days later, on a Sunday morning after a somber weekend of watching the nation get ready to bury their president, I saw Jack Ruby kill Lee Harvey Oswald live on television—as it was actually happening in the moment. I was stunned and over the next few years it seemed as if the country had devolved into chaos with Martin Luther King, Robert Kennedy, Vietnam and its protests. We had lost our innocence.

But the JFK assassination always haunted me. I watched the Zapruder film hundreds of times, and other documentaries and books that came out on the subject. I was fascinated with the controversies and the theories and all the conflicting evidence. I guess I always harbored doubts that it was a single shooter but there did not seem to be any concrete evidence for multiple shooters either—although there seemed to be substantial circumstantial evidence.

Over the years, then the decades that followed there was a restlessness there in my mind, that festers like a toothache until you finally go to the dentist and have it taken care of once and for all.

That is what ultimately happened and to me it indicates the power of visiting the actual site of an event. Recently I went to Dallas and there it all was— just like I had seen it on television and in pictures. Dealey Plaza, the Texas Schoolbook Depository, the grassy knoll, all relatively unchanged from the images I had seen. The first thing that struck me was how compact Dealey Plaza was. I imagined a much larger area but in reality it is quite a tight quartered area, surrounding the street like a small amphitheater surrounding a stage.

There were white "X"s on the street to designate where the motorcade was at the time of each of the three shots, that were fired from the fifth floor window of the school book depository. I stared for an indeterminately longer time at the third "X". That was the third shot that ended the life of a president and changed the course of history for millions of people all over the world.

Some fifty years after I had been a witness to the some of the events, I was standing on the spot where it actually happened. I cannot tell you how powerful a moment that was for me—it was like I went back in time and all the emotions and thoughts that I had accumulated over the years washed over me like a wave. I could not hold my emotions back. I cried the tears that I never did when I was a kid because I now had the full weight of the gravity of what occurred here behind me. But that was only the first of powerful moments I had that day.

The schoolbook depository is now a museum that has many exhibits and artifacts of the time. As I toured its floors, I was spell bound, until I came to the exhibit on the sixth floor. At the window where Lee Harvey Oswald allegedly fired the three shots in forty seconds, the scene had been set like it was back on that fateful day. There are boxes stacked around the window to conceal the shooter and boxes arranged in front of the window where the gunman could spread out and rest his shoulder to take his shots. It was a recreation of Lee Harvey Oswald's sniper nest.

I could picture him lying there, waiting nervously, looking, waiting as Kennedy's car came up and then turned onto Elm Street and started driving away. The crowd cheering and supposedly him the only one knowing what was about to happen or if it even would. And if it did the chaos that would ensue. The tension of those moments must have been almost unbelievable and yet he would have had to get it under control and stay cool enough to be able to accomplish his task.

As I stood there, I felt chills run up and down my spine. The ramifications of what the man who was right here at that moment—went back fifty years across a thousand miles, all the way back to a little kid in a fifth-grade classroom and later would stay with him the rest of his life. It was a seminal moment for me, one that I never expected, as it just kind of crept over me, but one that was indelible as I looked out that window and saw the same view that the assassin had that day.

It was if I was looking through the eyes of Lee Harvey Oswald seconds before he was about to pull the trigger and change the world. It was the second profound and powerful moment I had that day but there was one more to come. I exited the museum and went back down to the street, I wandered over to some cement structures on the side of the road. One was marked as the spot where Abraham Zapruder stood as he recorded one of the most significant films ever recorded.

Then I went over to the grassy knoll area. The fence area looked almost exactly as it appeared in 1963. Someone had placed an "X" on one of the fence boards. I knew what this "X" was intended to designate. This was not part of the government narrative. This was supposed to be the spot where it was claimed that a second shooter stood. It was this shooter who was to have fired the fatal third shot at JFK.

I peered over the fence.

In clear sight of this shooter's view loomed the "X" in the street. The place where the third shot struck JFK and ended his life. It was right there in front of me. The logistics of it all was right there. It took a few seconds and then wham—it hit me. One of the few epiphanies of my life but it was undeniable. I began to feel a strange calm come over me, a sense of release, a sense of peace, a sense of closure.

I played it out in my mind all the way back to my hotel and it made sense. It felt right, like putting the last pieces of a jigsaw puzzle together. It felt right, it felt complete. I muttered under my breath to myself, I think I finally figured out what happened here. At least to my way of thinking. I think I can finally put this to rest. I know this is going to sound funny because the assassination of JFK never prayed on my mind—to the point where it kept me awake at night but that night, I had one of the deepest most restful night's sleep of my life. Maybe it had always resided in my subconsciousness.

Here is what I figured out from my visit that day. I just want to say that this is only my theory and it may not work for anyone else, but I am thoroughly convinced that this is how it went down. I believe that there was a shooter in the window of the fifth floor of the schoolbook depository. However, I am not sure it was even Oswald. Oswald's famous statement "I'm just a patsy" lends some credence to that line of thinking. And that he was killed in order to silence him is also highly conceivable.

When I was in the sniper's den on the sixth floor and I looked at the sightline through the eyes of the sniper I asked myself one question, "Why did he wait?" First, let me qualify I am not an expert shooter. I have had a little gun training, I have been a hunter, and I have played in some recreational war games but when I asked this question— it was just from an average person's common-sense point of view.

Let me explain. The sixth-floor window had excellent views of two streets, Houston street and Elm street. On that day Kennedy's car came up Houston toward the Texas book depository at an estimated 20-25 miles per hour after it turned right off Main, then it slowed dramatically to 10 miles per hour or less right in front of the schoolbook depository. As it made a left onto Elm street slowly picking up speed it moved away from the sniper.

It has always been true even in my limited experience that a target that is moving towards you is infinitely easier to hit than a target that is moving away—but the sniper did not take that opportunity to shoot. Not only was Kennedy's car moving toward the sniper but it practical stopped and posed— like it was suspended in slow motion and pausing for a picture at the closest possible proximity to the shooter. If I did not know better, I would say that someone was presenting the president in the best target position possible, almost like when you have a deer in your sights, and it turns sideways giving the hunter the ideal shot. The sniper had that ideal situation with the president's car in precise a state of suspended animation at the base of the schoolbook depository building and still the sniper did not shoot.

He waited.

Now the car (Kennedy) was moving away and picking up speed—both adverse conditions to a successful strike. Finally, with the Kennedy car moving away from the sniper it is believed he fired his first shot, which missed everything and struck the road pavement. A second shot struck Kennedy and Governor Connelly via (the magic bullet) and the third shot was the furthest away from the schoolbook depository and the fatal shot to President Kennedy. Back to my question of why a shooter would wait for an option that had the least chance of success, before he opened fire.

If it was a lone shooter as the official record wants the public to believe he would have considered option one, with the target moving towards him as a more viable option, option two with the President almost stationary and in closest proximity as the ultimate option, but the sniper waited for the third option which guaranteed the least possible successful outcome.

The key lies in the fact the shooter was not alone and he knew it. That explains why he bypassed his first two options, because he was waiting for the President's car to get in the optimum position for multiple shooters to come into play. This makes sense and so to my mind I was convinced there was more than one shooter and at least two. That was confirmed in my mind when I peered over the fence at the grassy knoll.

That was the kill shot without a doubt. A target moving slowly in your direction right in the wheelhouse of your cross hairs. I knew then that it was a conspiracy to kill the President—no matter what I had been told to the contrary over the past fifty years. It was my moment of epiphany and it would never have occurred if I had not taken the time and effort to visit the site.

My final assessment of this matter that Kennedy was set up to enter this theatre (the intimate and enclosed area of the Dealey Plaza) which was to provide a kind of triangulation deathtrap. It was a killing zone which was designed to allow the President to enter but in which he would never be allowed to come out alive. I am convinced it was an organized premeditated assassination conspiracy. Who was responsible? I have my theories on that as well in a later section of this book.

The point of this is to illustrate that when a person is presented with a piece of information, they need to be able to assess it for themselves. They need to examine the sources and take into account possible motives. It would benefit them to do some independent investigation or research some other accounts and gather as much pertinent evidence as possible. A logical person would then take the evidence and analyze it and then make an informed decision. This is what critical thinking looks like and it allows you to synthesize information. It leads to intelligent, responsible and independent decisions.

What I'm about to say next is going to shock some people. Not only does the left wing of this country not care about the quality of education, even though they pretend to, they would prefer uneducated students. That is exactly what they want by *design*. The education system is just a microcosm for what the left wants to do to the rest of society.

It is no wonder that analysis and synthesis is not being taught in our schools because this is the last thing that the left wants. The last thing they want is to turn out independent, critical thinkers because that runs completely contrary to a low information voter. A person who can think for themselves is not likely to take a sound bite like "Trump is bad" and accept it on its face value. A critical thinker might want to investigate that statement and come to their own conclusion. And the left does not want to leave that conclusion to chance.

They do not want there to be any doubt that their constituents will deviate in any way from their dictates and not follow the party line. They want sheep to accept whatever they say as if it were the truth and go to the ballot box and pull the lever for whoever the left designates as their candidate every four years.

Does this sound like a vibrant democracy in action? It sounds more like a robotic Manchurian Candidate programmed to do the bidding of an elitist few, who in order to perpetuate its power will sacrifice whole generations of our youth.

It took me awhile, but I realized that liberals and the left who are running our school do not want critical thinkers coming out of their system. They want malleable sheep. Moreover, a process is needed to accomplish this. Therefore, they try to erase the history of the country and the ideals and principles that it was founded on. Then they replace these events with their own version, one that serves their agenda and espouses their beliefs and principals. Religion and families are bad so do not listen to them and the state will provide you with everything you need from cradle to grave.

The left has been very good at recognizing that the youth of this country was its future and they have been very successful in indoctrinating with its agenda, and the reward for all this hard work by the left is the kind of society we have now. Where our younger generation has a meltdown if they are faced with any type of adversity and political correctness is the rule and if you ask a young person who won the Civil War, all you get is crickets.

I have always said that liberals are specialists at creating captive audiences. That's the only way that most of the teachers in the school system have any students in their classroom, because the law requires them to be there. God forbid, that the DOE trained teachers to be interesting and engaging enough, that a student might want to attend their class of their own volition. I was in a seminar once, where the lecturer was telling a group of teachers how to be more engaging—and she delivered her instruction in the most monotone, uninspiring, disconnected presentation I have ever witnessed. Talk about teaching by example.

The education system is just a microcosm of what liberals will do when they get control of our lives. They want sheep who are dependent on them for everything and will do what they tell them to do without question.

But that is exactly the kind of product the left wants coming out of their liberal processing plants. When the process was just starting to evolve we used to call it the "dumbing down of America," now we call it a "special kind of stupid" but it goes beyond that. Liberals want to erase the values that this country was founded on, and replace them with their version of history because it does not fit their narrative, their own brand of ideals.

This was always the grand design.

The democrats would infiltrate the education system and foster in our youth this special kind of stupid (SKOS). Then along with the complicit media the Democratic party could promote their agenda, and nobody would question it, and they would parlay that special brand of stupidity into a perpetuity of power. If a liberal says something they want them to take it on face value and not question it. It must be true. The ultimate goal is to be able to tell you who to vote for and then they will always have power. But the cost is our freedom.

The Hunter and Joe Biden affair is a perfect example of how this special kind of stupid works. Hunter Biden was given lucrative deals to be on the boards of foreign energy companies not long after his father who was vice president at the time was put in charge of overseeing foreign affairs in the same countries that hired Hunter Biden.

The problem with this scenario is that Hunter Biden just happens to have no experience whatsoever, in energy. But what he does have is access to the vice presidency of the United States. So, the democrats president said there was nothing going on here. And remarkably everyone on the left takes those words at their face value. The complicit media who take their marching orders from the Democratic party (something that the election of Donald Trump has exposed completely) do not look into the affair to find the truth. Forasmuch as a legitimate news organization would be charged to do, they neglect the truth but print the propaganda that the democrats has proclaimed. If everything was on the up and up as Joe Biden claimed, then why did his son resign his position from the board shortly after the whole scam was exposed. No one on the left has ever dared to ask that question.

That is the problem when most of the press is in the leftist tank, a democrats is not used to responding to a real question because all they get are softballs. It is no wonder that Joe Biden is able to go on with his endless stories about how he was a lifeguard in his younger days, and he was able to save civilization from the likes of "Cornpop" and his gang. It is exactly this kind of treatment by the press that enables a Joe Biden to be a politician for what seems like hundreds of years and has never been on the right side of any issue. But to hear Biden tell it, he authored this legislation and that legislation and next thing he will have us believing that he wrote the Constitution (the left-wing press might fall for it because he appears to be old enough to have been there).Another former vice-president, Al Gore had us believing that he invented the internet. What is it about these vice presidents that they feel they have to make themselves seem more important than merely a second banana. They become LITOM (legends in their own minds.)

Case in point: Biden was asked a question by a reporter from a conservative entity for once, about his role in eliminating terrorist leaders. "Oh yeah, we did that with Osama Bin Laden." Apparently the reporter had a better memory than Biden and was not going to let Biden off the hook so easily. He retorted "Wasn't it true that you advised Obama against taking that action?" Biden responded "No".

However there is a video from that period of time where Biden states in his own words that he was against the assassination of Bin Laden. Revisionist history is such a wonderful tool if you are a democrat and your goal is to be a legend in your own mind.

How far this country has fallen.

I suppose that I could cite plenty of statistics that show how American is on the high end of spending money on education and how our students are on the lower end of the learning spectrum. We mentioned the Asian study earlier, but statistics are not needed to tell parents today what they already know. They are getting very little bang for their buck. The American education system is an abject failure and I can tell you is not an accident.

It is by design.

After 15 years of working in a profession that I loved, but in a system that I loathed, my advice is to never send your child to a public school. Send them to a charter school, home school them, encourage them to read on their own, travel with them whenever you can, anything, but don't send them to a public school.

Parents are increasingly taking responsibility for the education of their children and the trend to homeschooling is growing.

"By 2010 it was well over 3% and growing ever faster. Parents chose home schooling from the reasons that differ little from those that led another 4% of Americans to pay for private schooling and 7 percent to pay for religious (mostly Catholic) schooling. These are the same reasons why parents of public school children clamor for charter schools. In short, one out of seven sets of parents has already abandoned the public schools and many more wish they could.... Small rural public schools are a special case because parents can influence the content and standards of education. They typically have the lowest per pupil expenditures...and produce America's highest SAT scores." (The Ruling Class)

The internet has made homeschooling more user friendly. "The result is that SAT scores for home schoolers hover around the eightieth percentile. How did those dumb violent racists achieve results like that?" (The Ruling Class)

Consider this, liberals are "advocating a direct relationship between the government and children," effectively abolishing the presumption of parental authority. Hence, whereas within living memory school nurses could not administer an aspirin to a child without the parents' consent, the people who run America's schools nowadays administer pregnancy tests and ship girls off to abortion clinics without the parent's knowledge." (The Ruling Class) There was an incident on the news recently where a first-grade class was discussing Santa Claus. Of course, it was not unexpected that at such an early age many of these students still believed in Santa Claus. Apparently, this first-grade teacher felt it was her place to set the record straight when she proclaimed, "Your parents are liars." This should send chills down the spine of every parent who has a child in the school system.

So, mission accomplished. The college graduates of today are dumb as a rock, brainwashed of American principles, taught to hate our country and programmed to accept the marching orders from the left without question. Phase I is complete. The table is set. Phase II is to find a complicit accomplice.

In the end what did we learn from our foray into the workings of the education system?

Someone who can think is a danger to themselves.

Someone who can question and think is a danger to the state.

"We don't need no mind control"

"Teacher leave those kids alone"

New World Order

"You can vote Communism in, but you will have to shoot your way out." (Facebook meme)

This is where it all came together for me, not really as an epiphany but as a series of trial and error experiences, questioning and applying some critical thinking, to where I was able to assemble all the pieces of the puzzle, until they fit—or at least made sense to me. There was not really an "aha" moment, unlike my Kennedy revelation which I describe earlier, in that 50 years of examination and research had culminated in a transcendent moment when I visited the assassination site.

In contrast to the Kennedy situation, I was much more of a pawn in the perpetration of the education myth. I actually worked for the Department of Education for many years even though to them, I was just another a piece on the system's chessboard, one of many that they had successfully bamboozled and manipulated. Until there was a point, when I had what I would call an awakening. I puzzled for a number of years over the DOE's policies and modus operandi. A lot of the things they did seemed to run counter-productive to what should be expected of an educator in the teaching profession. Why are they not teaching our kids American values, to be independent, to be more analytical in their way of thinking? I kept banging my head against the wall until eventually the lightbulb came on.

THEY DON'T WANT TO. It is part of their *design*.

Only then did it begin to make some sense. I'm sure that there are a lot of people who get into teaching who have good intentions as I did. However, they are being played as I was and they haven't figured it out yet or they have figured it out and they are content to go along with the program, perhaps because they bought into the program long before they became a teacher.

It was never *my* program and so I was always a skeptic. Some thought I was just jaded, but it was more than that. I was unconvinced, resistant and defiant. The question I kept asking myself, became my gold standard.

To what end?

When I applied this question, the answers started to come, so I kept applying it. It is especially helpful when you take the forty-thousand foot view and scope out the whole landscape. So let's do that. Let's go up in the plane and do an exercise in IFTTT, (If this, then that).

Why is the system not teaching our kids traditional American values? *To what end?* So that they can replace them with a more leftist agenda.

Why is the system not teaching our kids to think critically? *To what end*? So that they will not be able to think independently, and they will accept what leftists tell them and accept it without question.

Why does the education system want to produce malleable students who have been exposed to left wing values? To what end? So that they will become malleable citizens predisposed to left wing values.

Why do they want to transfer the microcosm they have created in the classroom to the laboratory of society? *To what end?* Because it translates to power. The power they hold over the educational system will be Democratic political power in the public sector. A herd of sheep predisposed to left wing values, dependent on Democratic socialist handouts and shepherded by a corrupt and complicit media is an easily controlled and formidable voting bloc. And ultimately a pathway to power. Power is always the ultimate goal. Power trumps everything.

Here is the formula that encapsulates the leftist road to achieving power.

Indoctrination+Dependence=Control=Power

I like to characterize the leftist world view versus the conservative world view in this manner. Let's say you have two cats; one is a domesticated house cat and the other is a wild feral cat. The feral cat is out in the wild, hunting and foraging for its survival. It is not dependent on anyone and it is free to hunt when, what and where it wants. No one controls it therefore no one has power over it. It enjoys its natural God-given freedom.

The house cat, on the other hand, is dependent on its masters for food, water, shelter and medical care. It enjoys no freedom and is a "captive" (it's funny how this word keeps popping up when there is a reference to the left) in its artificial environment. It has become accustomed to the illusion of security, but it is wholly at the mercy and the benevolence or the malevolence of its master.

And the cat had no say in the choosing of its master. It is dependent on the master for the basic necessities of life. The master controls its destiny, therefore the master has the power of life and death. If the domesticated cat were to seek its freedom in the wild, it would most likely die because it doesn't have the natural ability that it was born with, to survive.

Is this not an adequate analogy of the incestuous education, media, Democratic Party, socialism symbiotic relationship? One feeding off the other.

Couple cases in point. Democratic presidential candidate Kamala Harris once proposed a ten hour school day. It caused a modicum of controversy at the time it was announced. Rebecca Friedrichs was interviewed as opposing this measure. She has been a strong advocate against teachers' unions purportedly because they do not have our kid's best interests at heart. Her argument is that more time at school is just more time to brainwash our kids, make them completely dependent on the State for meals, medical, what they will learn, and make their parents irrelevant in the development of their lives.

I agree with her and I saw this firsthand as a teacher in New York City. We had very few snow days because the school was everything—even babysitter—and parents were at a loss about what to do with their own kids if they were not in school. And that's what the school is intending to be—surrogate parents. The nanny state. From morning to night. They are essentially striving to be glorified babysitters. And they don't even do a good job at that. They make great dysfunctional babysitters.

When Barak Obama was elected president in 2008, people of color and democrats were delirious, and they had a right to be. He was the first black president. I was a little more reserved in my judgement and it had nothing to do with skin color. I knew very little about the man. Just a few years before he was a relatively unknown community organizer and had come out of nowhere to be elected president of the United States. It seemed to be such a precipitous ascent in such a short period of time. I also wanted to see him in action before I graded his work. There was no doubt that he was an eloquently spoken man, but words are one thing and deeds are another. Let's see what he does.

A few weeks into his administration, somehow, he won a Nobel Peace Prize. I'm not sure even he knows to this day what he did to justify it. How could anybody produce a body of work in a matter of weeks that was significant enough to be worthy of such a prestigious award? Others have worked lifetimes for such an honor. Now I began to get suspicious.

Four years later I knew everything that I needed to know, and it had nothing to do with skin color. The US economy was in dismal shape, our deficit and national debt were sky-rocketing and our military was in one of its weakest state of affairs, despite being involved in conflicts all around the globe. Just on that record alone, one could have safely assumed that this was going to be a one term presidency. But this president still talked a good game—good enough to get re-elected in 2012.

At this point, I began applying my gold standard litmus test again. To every policy that Obama tried to enact, I measured it against the question—"Is this the best thing for the country?" The only thing that ever passed the test was the assassination of Osama Bin Laden. On virtually every other issue from declining the XL pipeline at a time when we were in need of both energy and jobs, to sending billions of dollars to Iran when we were in debt and Iranians were screaming "death to America" as they were developing nuclear capabilities, Obama seemed to be on the other side. In fact, completely on the other side, like 180 degrees on the other side.

President Obama always impressed me as being a fairly intelligent man but some of these proposals were of breath-taking stupidity. Not even a special kind of stupid does it justice. So what is any rational human being left to conclude? The only thing they can conclude in the face of such evidence:

It was intentional.

How can I say such a thing? That an American president was intentionally trying to sabotage the country from within. It is not such a hard preposition when we go back to the 40,000 foot view and look at the scenery from a global scope and ask our question again "To what end?"

America is the biggest obstacle to globalism. Other countries have opened their borders to a flood of immigrants, have adopted socialistic, environmentalist policies and anti-nationalistic principles. America has continued to cling to its founding principles of freedom and capitalism, but barely by its fingernails. God forbid, if Obama had retained control of the House and the Senate during his second term in office. They were the only checks and balances that prevented him from wreaking complete havoc on our country and the Constitution at the time. But not to worry, they had Hillary Clinton waiting in the wings to finish the job. It was all rigged so that she would assume the throne and continue the transformation of America. How else do you explain the predetermined primary with Bernie Sanders and the superdelegates? Many people say she stole the nomination.

And how do you explain the fixed investigation on Hillary with her illegal private server and her bleached-bit emails? Emails that had been under subpoena. The same people who were in on the exoneration fix of Hillary Clinton were the same people who were generating a Russian collusion hoax against Donald Trump. The Jim

Comeys, the Peter Strzoks and the Lisa Pages of the word. And how do you explain Bill Clinton meeting with attorney general Loretta Lynch on an airport tarmac while his wife was under an investigation? If that is not a conflict of interest and the appearance of impropriety, I don't know what is. All this to what end? Because it is impossible for anyone to rule the country from a jail cell.

But then something happened.

The problem was that, against all odds, something, nothing short of a miracle, shocked them to their core. They lost the election. The plan to take America down from the inside was derailed, at least temporarily. And make no mistake about it, America *has* to be taken down in the globalist scheme of things. America must be diminished for globalism to be fully implemented. It is too much of a beacon of light.

It explains why the reputation of America is constantly tarnished and denigrated. America was regarded as the greatest country in the world, but we are not perfect. To be honest, we have made mistakes in the past, but many mistakes were in the context of the times. The rest of the world was doing the same thing, or in many cases, far worse. And yet Barack Obama felt compelled to go on an apology tour in his first term as president.

Immigrants are taught to hate this country even as they seek to come here to live and to take refuge. It really is an amazing phenomena. They will risk their lives to come to our shores and enjoy the benefits of our economy and our freedom and then in the same breath, they use their freedom to condemn us and idolize the place that they just escaped from. It truly is a sight to behold. They don't appreciate our country and they don't respect our laws and they don't make any attempt to assimilate.

Congresswoman Ilhan Omar is a perfect example. She was in a refugee camp in her country and her life was in extreme peril. She was granted asylum and came to the United States. We offered her safety, financial support and freedom. She parlayed that into political power, which would have been unthinkable in her home country and yet she is prominent voice in the castigation of America.

We are constantly lectured (a specialty of leftists in general and Obama in particular) about how America should try to emulate Europe. The last time I looked Europe wasn't doing that well with high unemployment, inflation and plenty of immigration consequences. Why would we want to emulate those failed policies unless we wanted to replicate the same kind of detrimental results?

We are told that we must align with global protocols regarding the environment. America's leftist Green New Deal must be implemented or we are facing extinction in 12 years. However, it has been revealed that some proponents of this scare tactic admit that this course of action is less about saving the environment and more about the distribution of wealth. America must be taken down.

"While the Ruling Class prods Americans to become more like Europeans and talks as if Americans should move up to 'world standards' the Country Class believes that America's ways are superior to the rest of the world's and regards most of mankind as less free, less prosperous and less virtuous than American." (The Ruling Class)

By contrast, say whatever you want about Donald Trump, but one thing is indisputable—that he loves the United States of America and he put the country first. He passes the gold standard test—"what is best for the country?" and again, say what you want about his style, but the results have been nothing less than spectacular. His economy might be the best in the history of the country.

At one point during his campaign, Trump criticized the Obama administration for their loss of manufacturing jobs to companies overseas and claimed that if he was elected president he would reverse this trend. Obama condescendingly alluded, that this was the new normal and derided Trump by saying "what was he going to do, wave a magic wand?" Maybe in lieu of a wand, all Trump really needed was the *desire* to do something that was in the best interests of the country.

Donald Trump has thrown a giant unexpected monkey wrench into the gears of the globalist machinery. And this is becoming more evident with each passing day. The election of Donald Trump has exposed the true nature of the democrats, the media, and the deep state for the rest of the country to see. The America, as the sovereign traditional country that we once knew, was on life support, before Trump got elected and he almost single handedly resuscitated it.

He has rolled back the globalist agenda far more than they would have ever expected. Trump is their worst nightmare. And that is why there is such hatred for him. It is called Trump Derangement Syndrome and it is attributed to the Democratic Party in America because he defeated them in the election. How can there be such hatred for a president who is achieving such unprecedented positive results for the country? The left has even extended their hatred to include all conservatives and anyone who ever voted for Trump.

Honestly, I think that Trump Derangement Syndrome is just a cover for the movement of globalism. He is an obstacle in their path of a new world order and so are the people who support him and voted him into power. He stands in their way. Conservatives stand in their way. And an America in the control of Republicans stand in their way.

The 40,000 ft view starts with education and ends with globalism. In between, the plan is to demonize Trump, demonize his supporters and bring down America. Some say the plan doesn't end there and it goes beyond globalism. Listen folks, I never claimed to be a genius or a prophet or have any special skills of divination. I'm just an ordinary guy who was an educator for 15 years teaching history. But I've also been around long enough to know when it feels right. And this fits. Only when the pieces of the puzzle are put together in this manner it does seem to make sense. It was just like the Kennedy experience that I had. It all went together and made sense—at least to me. That's the scheme in a nutshell. Sometimes you don't need all the facts. Sometimes you don't need all the details. Sometimes you just know a thing is right.

What is this globalism anyway? This new world order? This one world order? It all seems very vague to me. When I start hearing those terms, I start imagining some kind of 1984- esque, soulless, desolate society, of dependence on government, with Big Brother as the totalitarian leader, I guess. Maybe my concept is not that far off. To me, 1984 paints about as bleak a picture of society as I can imagine— and yet let us not forget that it is based on actual conditions under Fascism and Communism, regimes that exist in places today. However, one thing I am certain of is that the light of America is the only thing that stands between us and the darkness of that world.

When they extinguish that light—God help us all.

I mean that literally. There are people who take this to a higher level, a spiritual level—one of prophecy. And end times prophecy does not include any prominent mention of the United States of America.

It does mention a powerful antichrist.

And an Armageddon.

A Leftist Manifesto for Control of the Masses (based on the playbook of the Third Reich)

Education

Purge the school system from college professors to public school teachers of any educators who espouse a dissenting or opposite viewpoint.

Erase the events of past history that don't fit the narrative.

Allow for a period of time in order that people will forget what really happened.

Rewrite or modify history to fit the narrative and only teach that version. Repeat this for all subjects in the curriculum.

Remove any references to God and especially Christianity from the classroom.

Replace religion with the state or the environment.

Discourage or ban any free speech or opposing voices.

Get children into the system as early as possible and keep them as long as possible.

Make the school the state-the be all end all that children and their parents become dependent on.

Supplant the parents as the authority in the children's lives.

Do not let children become critical or independent thinkers. Discourage creativity and individualism of any kind.

Place the highest value on conformity and teach them to obey and follow like sheep-without question.

Teach them to make decisions based on emotions-not reason or logic.

Pretend that you care about them.

Media

Completely disregard any previous mandates to present the public with the truth.

If there is no evidence to support your narrative—fabricate it—if and whenever necessary as long as it advances your agenda.

Ban or eliminate any dissenting viewpoints.

Promote your political agenda.

Only present one side of the story in the best light possible.

EPIPHANY

Thoughts on Globalism

"What keeps it all together? What is the denominator, the common thread that somehow, unites us all?"

I surmised that it was something that reaches pretty deep and far back because the disparate nature of our country didn't happen overnight, either. It has been there from the beginning, as well.

After some retrospection, with some help from a previous career as a teacher and historian, I concluded that there was one element that has transcended all physical boundaries, ideologies, economic disparities and even time, itself. And that was the 'spirit of freedom' (something that, sadly, is seldom taught in our schools anymore.)

This is a country that was founded on that spirit. "conceived in liberty", was how Lincoln phrased it. It's in our blood. It's in our DNA.

Freedom of religion brought the first settlers to our shores and their God-based spirit of freedom is the very soul of our country. Some, in their efforts to rewrite our history assert that the early settlers came to this land for gold. Some of the explorers and the conquistadors surely did. But the first settlers who came to American soil came to escape religious persecutions in other countries. To this day I have never heard of a gold mine being discovered in Massachusetts. The only gold they sought was the freedom to practice their religion in the way that they saw fit. That Christian ethos became the foundation upon which this country was built no matter how much the progressives try to recast it or deny it. Religion was integral at the time of our inception, it has preserved this country through perilous times, and unfortunately, I fear, it will be our downfall. Because it has systematically been removed from our public schools so it can be replaced by the nanny state.

There is no doubt that we are a unique country; one that is exceptional in the history of the world, (something else that is no longer taught in our schools, but rather, the very opposite-that we should be apologists). That the country is racist (1619 Project and Critical Race Theory) and it should be condemned. Our public schools are teaching our students to hate this country in yet another effort to topple it from within.

Up to the time of our declaration of independence and the beginning of the great American experiment, the civilizations and societies of the world were run by kings and dictators who derived their power from their bloodline, or by brute force. Once in power, they instituted systems that were designed to keep the masses of people (or subjects as they were known) under their submission and keep themselves in power.

The average peasant was not free to do as he or she pleased. He/she was subservient to the king and he/she did the king's bidding or faced consequences, some of which could be extremely dire, depending on the discretion of the king. The peasant was told what his/her role in life would be, and he/she had little choice in the matter.

This kind of authority would eventually evolve into caste systems and feudal systems and other hierarchies of labor and servitude, designed to perpetuate the power structure and keep control of the population from birth to death. The most determining factor, one that determined your fate in this kind of society, for the rest of your life was, who your parents were. It was as if you were a breed of dog.

Some regimes were more oppressive than others and ran the gamut from socialism to communism to slavery (sometimes it was hard to distinguish one from the other). Under any of these systems, few people were free to determine their own fate and there was no such thing as elections. That concept would be inconceivable to a medieval serf.

The discovery of America changed all that. It offered an interesting alternative to people who rejected the tyranny, of having to live a life in a system in which someone, with no other qualifications than their lineage, got to dictate how you were to live every aspect of your life.

People saw an opportunity to escape that kind of oppressive dominance, albeit, at great risk and peril to their own existence. There was a high likelihood that it might require you to pay the ultimate price. However, death is rarely a deterrent to someone imbued with the spirit of freedom, and that is a theme we will see repeatedly, throughout the course of this writing. In fact, it was the message stamped on the front and back of our car, that we carried with us to all the other states, that we visited on our recent excursion. It's a sentiment that everyone who lives and drives a car in New Hampshire sees, on a daily basis. Our license plates proudly proclaim it, "Live Free or Die" for anyone who cares to take note.

It honors how precious that sentiment was to those that risked their lives to come to these shores and how badly they craved freedom. It was their chance to be able to speak their own language, to be free to express themselves, to worship who and how they wanted and to conduct their life in a manner they deemed fit. "They" became the operative word. "They" would get to decide.

And so, America became "the great experiment" where the power, for the first time in the history of human civilization, was entrusted to the people ("of the people, by the people, for the people".) For the first time, it was "the people" who decided their own fate and it ran radically, contrary to everything that had preceded it. No more kings! No more despots! There would be elections to determine the "will" of the people.

This is all very important because it goes to the heart of a country that was founded on these principles. If freedom is the soul of this country, the Constitution and the principles and institutions it embodies, are the heart of our country. A country, where a man is measured by his merits and judged by his accomplishments; not the color of his skin or who his parents were.

In fact, what mattered most was what an individual did and not who he was. *That*, is what made America unique and exceptional. We embraced this experiment based on the spirit of freedom, and while it has never been perfect, that spirit and the ingenuity and the entrepreneurship that it unleashed, made us the wealthiest, most powerful nation in the world.

One of my favorite movies is Braveheart. I have always wondered why I was so fascinated with this film, and I surmise it is because it so embodies the spirit of freedom. The Scottish people fought and died, so that their country might be free of English rule. However, while that might have been important to the Scots it was not even close to the kind of freedom that America envisioned. On closer inspection, it is true, that the Scots would not have to contend with rule under an English monarch, but they would still be governed by the rule of a Scottish king. And while that might be *less* oppressive, it still didn't deliver any rights to the individual. In that sense, it was a poor imitation of the American brand of freedom.

American freedom is as exceptional as the country itself. Patrick Henry once expressed the essence of the Americanization of freedom in a few simple words, "Give me liberty or give me death." I don't know if this would have made it to a license plate even if there were cars back then. This was not exactly a benign proclamation when you consider that he was issuing it to the face, of the most powerful nation in the world, at the time. A rebel, if caught, was more than likely to be given the back end of that choice.

One of the most incredible stories that I have ever read, was in Edward Burrows ground-breaking "Forgotten Patriots", that tells the horrendous story of the American prisoners who were captured by the British in the Revolutionary War. In the duration of that war, some 200,000 Americans fought against our British foes. Approximately 6,800 soldiers died in battle. What is incredible, is that it has been estimated, that as many as 32,000 American patriots may have been captured by British forces and that 11,000 to 16,000 may have died in captivity. If we accept the higher estimate, that is almost three times the number of men that died in actual battle.

During that time, American prisoners of war were generally brought to New York, by the British, who used that city as the base of their military operations in colonies. Once there, they were housed in whatever facilities were available, (usually old warehouses or sugar houses). However, when these spaces were filled, the British began employing old hulks of warships and anchoring them in Wallabout Bay.

The conditions in the holds of these ships, were some of the cruelest and most inhumane ever perpetrated on fellow human beings. Thousands of men would be crammed into spaces, that were only meant to accommodate a few hundred. Rations were rancid at best and unsustainable for anything, but slow starvation at worst. The men below decks were covered in lice and human excrement. Disease was rampant and it decimated these prisoners, at the rate of 70% in some cases.

The part that is truly incomprehensible about this situation, is that if you took an oath to join the Loyalist movement, you were immediately released from these hellish dungeons. In some cases, you did not even have to swear allegiance to the crown, but just promise not to take up arms against the British, if you were released. It was literally a decision that held life and death in the balance. Few prisoners took the British up on their offer and approximately 16,000 chose to die, for the freedom of their country.

"So wedded were they to their principals, so dear to them was their country, so true were they to their honor, that rather than sacrifice them, they preferred the scoffs of their persecutors, the horrors of their dungeon, and in fact even death itself."

Edwin Burrows, "Forgotten Patriots"

It was the ultimate example of what an American was willing to endure, in the name of freedom.

How inspirational, that, here was a country that had that kind of spirit of freedom incorporated into its cornerstones. How was it possible that a country, infused with such an endemic devotion to patriotism, could ever *not* succeed?

And so, I wondered about that too. There have been many great civilizations of the world and the one thing they all have in common, is that they all collapsed or disappeared. From the Greeks, Egyptians and Romans to the Mayas, Incas and Aztecs of the Americas, they all fell for one reason or another-whether it was attributed to internal strife or external forces of nature.

I am afraid that this same fate will befall this great American empire of ours, as well. My wife tells me that America does not play a very prominent role in the end times prophecy. In fact, it hardly garners much mention at all. Although no one knows exactly when this apocalypse will occur and seeing firsthand the greatness that we have achieved as a nation, it hardly seems possible that we could suffer such a precipitous decline.

But there is no denying that there are many precedents.

And our cracks are beginning to show.

As recent as 10 years ago, I would have scoffed at such a suggestion and if such a calamity were to befall us, there would have been no doubt whatsoever, that it would have been something foisted on us from some outside entity or foreign incursion. But in the last 10 years, it has become far more conceivable, that our downfall will be of an internal genesis.

"We" are likely to be the cause of our own downfall.

To underscore this, it was the same thing that was foreseen by Lincoln before the Civil War.

"America will never be destroyed from the outside. If we falter and lose our freedoms, it will be because we destroyed ourselves."

My fear is that the spirit of freedom, which was the source of our birth as a nation will also be the ultimate source of our demise.

Education has been tabbed as the building block for the destruction of freedom and exceptionalism. When I had my epiphany about critical thinking and why I was being castigated for teaching it. I couldn't understand it. I thought critical thinking was the purpose of education. When I realized that the purpose of education had been redesigned for just the opposite, then it all made sense. The purpose of education is to teach students not to think for themselves so that they can become more easily submissive. They are being conditioned to do what they are told and not question it. In more recent times education is the tool the left is using to indoctrinate our kids to hate this racist country. And to their credit it is working.

A recent poll conducted in the wake of the Ukrainian invasion by Russia asked what Americans would do if the United States was similarly invaded. Of people over 60 years old, 70% said they would stay and defend their country despite their advancing age. In the 45 to 60 age group, the percentage that would stay and fight dropped to 52%. In the age group of 18 to 45 the prime fighting age 70% said they would flee and abandon our country. Those numbers are the culmination of years of indoctrinating students to hate this country.

In summary that is the plan for our education. Take God out of the schools. Do NOT teach our children to think independently. Dumb them down so that they are compliant with what they are told. Obliterate our history and rewrite it with propaganda that destroys our ideals of exceptionalism and patriotism and replaces them with racism and hate. In essence the left has created a capitulant permanent voting bloc for the Democrat Party. One that will permanently cement their power.

But in the big picture education is only one part of the equation. The corporate media is enlisted to disseminate the propaganda of the Democratic Party. They broadcast the lies and agenda of left and provide the marching orders for the bovine-like electorate. The mainstream media by abandoning their responsibilities to supply the truth to an informed electorate have instead all but ensured the entrenchment of power for one party. Elitist democrats.

I was never much of a believer in the globalist and one world ideologies until I read George Orwell's 1984 again and began to realize how prophetic it really was. I was told at the book store that I purchased my copy that over the last few years the demand for this book has increased dramatically. Lots of people are reading it again because they are beginning to recognize the truth that is buried within its pages.

To me it is my vision of a globalist one world concept. Simply for those who have not read it, it describes a three tiered society not unlike that which dominated civilization until America came along and broke the mold. 1984 has the proles on the bottom. The proles represent the poorest individuals in society. They do the most unwanted menial forms of labor. All societies have this element and throughout most of history they were enslaved labor until that was abolished. They are uneducated and highly dependent on the classes above them. They are usually deemed no threat to the ruling class.

The next layer of society is the middle class. These are the working people and small business owners. In past societies it included, the tradesmen, artisans, and apprentices. They are more educated and more independent and because of this they are the real threat to the ruling class. In 1984, they have been virtually destroyed. They still exist but they have been brought to submission by an oppressive ruling class that manipulates, controls and surveils every aspect of their lives to keep them powerless. The live barely subsistent lives. They are forbidden to congregate speak out or think thoughts that are anti regime-est. The slightest sign of resistance is detected and eliminated.

The top layer of course is the elite. They have all the power and they determine the rules for the rest of the society but for which they themselves are exempt. Their power is absolute and they tolerate no threats to it. In the past this has always been the kings, the dictators and the oligarchs. Never a republic by the people for the people of the people. That was us. We were the exception. We were the first. We were uniquely American. Even today we are still a relatively rare entity. There are some other democracies but many of these are socialist. Most of the current world is either communist or socialist.

America is the last bastion of democracy and those principles are being eroded every day from outside and more recently from within. The American middle class is the obstacle to the globalist one world order. We must be destroyed. And we are being destroyed from within by the democrat party who want to be the power brokers for this new world. They use everything as a pretense to this end.

They have used the pandemic to invoke emergency powers to lock down America and destroy its economic system. They issued millions of dollars in relief aid to make America dependent on the government. The government spent money they didn't have and so they just printed more which triggered inflation further decimating our economy. Because they issued so much compensation money, people were making a lot more to stay home than to work even though there were millions of open jobs. Employers were forced to shut down their businesses because they couldn't find workers. Small businesses –the backbone of our economic engine—were particularly hard hit.

The liberals used the pandemic and the shutdowns to alter the voting procedures for the 2020 election. Mail in ballets were prevalent and led to a massive breach of integrity. Many believe that the liberals stole the 2020 election.

When the pandemic threat started to wane, there was further fear mongering concerning variants. When the variants proved to be less deadly, there was our involvement in a war in Ukraine.

Many believe that the democrats facing huge losses at the voting booth in 2022 will use any and all of these means to steal the election. I agree with that assessment, but I fear that they may employ martial law as a means to rig the voting process.

They have gained control of their constituents through indoctrination and propaganda. So only half the country remains a threat to their new world order and those are the conservatives. The real last bastion of real conservatism is the America First Trump voters. We are the only thing standing in their way. We must be destroyed at any cost by any means.

Joe Biden had a slogan in his 2020 presidential campaign, that the 2020 election was a "battle for the soul of the country". If that sentiment was true in 2020 it was never truer in the next 2 upcoming elections, the midterms in 2022 and the presidential election in 2024.

Not only is it a battle for the soul, the next two elections will be an existential battle for conservatives and the principles that our country was founded on. It is the last chance for conservatives to push back on the globalist agenda, one world ideology and preserve the sovereignty of our nation, at least for the time being.

We have seen what has happened in our country in just the first year of the Biden administration. Our rights as citizens under the Constitution have been under constant assault. Honest hardworking tax paying parents are being branded as terrorists for expressing an opinion. Our country is in economic chaos domestically and a laughing stock on the world stage. No one could have imagined this. In only one year. No one could have imagined that it could have happened so fast. In just one year our country is becoming unrecognizable.

If Conservatives don't win the election, it will be lost forever. This is not hyperbole and it is not an exaggeration. The globalists have a plan for us. They must fundamentally change the United States as we know it. Their plan is to put in place an elite class who will rule by tyranny. In order to do so they must destroy the middle class in this country. One half of the middle class is already in their pocket. The other half—the conservatives—has to be destroyed. They cannot be allowed to come back to power.

The globalists cannot afford to lose either of the next 2 elections. It would damage their agenda tremendously. And they certainly can never allow Donald Trump to come back to power in 2024 and reverse what they have accomplished so far. That would be disastrous. What will they do? What will we do? I think the left is prepared to throw everything including the kitchen sink at us in order to stay in power. How will we respond? I think the next 2 years determines the fate of this country once and for all. If nothing else it is going to be very interesting to say the least.

If and when the globalists ever gain control 1984 will be our future.

Read it and weep.

"If you want a picture of the future, imagine a boot stamping on a human face—forever." 1984 George Orwell.

Just before this book went to publication, it was announced that Elon Musk had acquired Twitter. He stated that he was a first amendment absolutist, and he did not agree with the censorship algorithms that the previous leftist owners had imposed on what he referred to as a "digital town square." According to Musk who is not a conservative by the way, his aim in buying Twitter was to restore all legal free speech in accordance with the constitution so that everyone's free speech is protected.

The left which owns every other digital platform went absolutely apoplectic over this turn of events. You would have thought that Musk had committed murder. First, they ridiculed him according to the liberal SOP (standard operating procedure.) Then they called him every name in the book from Hitler on down to a racist born in an apartheid South Africa as per step 2 of cancel culture SOP. They screamed that it was the end of democracy in the world. How is it that protecting the first amendment rights of free speech one of the tenets that democracy in America is founded on is the destruction of that very democracy?

Democrat politicians were claiming that it was unfair for one person to own a public forum such as Twitter but none of these democrats said a word when Jack Dorsey owned it. And he was the one that was censoring dissenting opinions. That was okay though because it was mostly conservatives that were being censored. These same democrats don't say anything about Mark Zuckerberg or Jeff Bezos, or George Soros.

The hypocrisy and the lunacy of such the firestorm the left created is mind boggling.

Immediately after the acquisition of Twitter the left weaponized their agencies such as the IRS and the FBI and launched investigations into Musk's business dealings in order to threaten, intimidate, cancel and destroy this man. Mind you this is the same man who was a hero to the left when he was developing his electric car company Tesla and his space company SpaceX. But because he became a proponent for free speech, suddenly, he became the devil.

Shortly after Musk's acquisition, the Department of Homeland security announced that they would be creating a Disinformation Governance Board to monitor content on digital platforms. This is right out of 1984 and the Ministry of Truth. You can bet your bottom dollar that the only thing that is going to be monitored and deemed disinformation is conservative dissent. These are the same people that have created an open southern border in which hundreds if not thousands of terrorists have gained entry into our country. These same people have decided that actual terrorists are less of a threat to our country than supporting the first amendment.

This tells you everything that you need to know about the left and their cancel culture mentality. They are against open forums for debate. They are against opposing viewpoints. They are against finding out the truth. They are for suppression, silencing, banning, censoring, cancelling, and destroying opposition opinion. That is how they got into power and how they plan to stay in control. They are terrified of free speech because it is a threat to their control.

This is America and freedom and the right to express your opinions are embroidered in tis fabric.

We must not let the left destroy these principles.

Recently a soldier was heard echoing this sentiment,

"Once I would have given my life for the principles that this country stood for; now I would give my life to fight against what this country has become."

That a stunning reversal! How did it come to this?

For everything that the leftists did to individuals such as myself and DB and others the real casualty of the cancel culture has been the "truth" itself. The destruction of truth was their ultimate goal. It seems like the democrats are bent on erasing over 400 years of history in 400 days.

After the 2016 election of Donald Trump we saw the mainstream media in this country finally take off their masks and expose themselves for the left wing, biased and dishonest haters and propagandists that they really were. There was no more pretense of objective journalism, not even a semblance. It was blatant distortion of truth, manipulation and oft-times complete omission of facts, and outright lies and fabrication. Just look at the names some of these newspapers give themselves such as Guardian and Sentinel—as if they are the paragons of seeking the truth for the American people—when in reality they are just shills for the Democratic Party.

An entity that had been founded on the principle of reporting the truth, which had been referred to as the fourth estate and had been entrusted with being the watchdog for the American people had abdicated its responsibility to democracy and the American Republic. The mainstream media had devolved into naked propagandists for the leftwing movement in general, and the Democratic Party in particular, and they do not deny it. In fact, they proudly proclaim it. It was a death knell for truth in this country. Donald Trump called them the "enemy of the people" because of their "fake news" and exposing the true nature of the news media was one of his greatest legacies. He had been one of the first to see it and had been sounding the fire bell on this way before the rest of us recognized it to be true.

Other than removing the integrity of our election system nothing is more destructive to the foundation of our democracy than a dishonest press. The role of the press in a democracy is to inform the constituency of the truth so that they can make educated decisions about their governance. Decisions made on the basis of untruths or without the truth are flawed and leave us as a nation vulnerable to destruction, both from outside forces and from within. That is the position that a press that is not free or fair has put this country in. Trump was never more prescient when he declared that "the press is the enemy of the people." He knew this to be true because he saw what the opposition did with the phony Russian collusion investigation. He knew personally that he had not colluded with the Russians and he had to endure an investigation in which the only evidence was a manufactured Russian dossier that was funded by his opponent in the 2016 election, Hillary Clinton.

He saw how the media took the Democrat Party's word for its' authentication, did not investigate on their own, and amplified the unsubstantiated claims to the American public. He had a front row seat to their lies. He saw first-hand not only what they did but what they were capable of. In the end, the death of truth at the hand of the American media will be the destruction the country itself.

"The Party told you to reject the evidence of your eyes and ears. It was their final and most essential command." 1984

But there was another phenomenon that arose from this fake news manipulation. It was termed the "are you going to believe your lying eyes/ears or what I tell you" syndrome. As an offshoot to the arrogance of the left, they no longer feel it is necessary for them to debate issues. They believe that they are right and that if you don't agree with them you are either wrong, ignorant, racist or other forms of name calling or deserving of censorship. This has evolved into a leftist mantra that if I say it is true it must be true even if I don't have any facts to back it up.

And because of this, conservatives on the other side of the argument are left to scratch their heads and mutter,

"Just because some says it does not make it true."

It has gotten so bad that leftists will lie right to our faces and with the evidence staring us right in our eyes and try to tell us that we are not really seeing or hearing what is right in front of us. The term for this is gaslighting- meaning.

A blatant example of this occurred when a CNN reporter was standing in front of a BLM riot with a building ablaze in the background and a war zone going on all around him and claimed that it was a "peaceful" demonstration. Because the audience on the left has been trained to act like sheep and not question what they are told the reporter is allowed to get away with this. No one on the left points out that the emperor has no clothes. When a conservative audience sees the same scenario, their reaction is to laugh and say,

"What kind of idiots do they think we are"?

A second example is the birth of the "Let's go Brandon" slogan. As it became more and more evident that the policies of Biden's first year in office were becoming utter failures, many people including Biden voters were losing face in the competence of the Biden administration. There was a lot of buyer remorse and it gave rise to people at concerts and sporting events showing their anger by chanting F---(expletive) Joe Biden.

Of course, the liberal mainstream media would not report on this in order to cover for Biden's failing regime and would cut away whenever the chant was happening. However, in one instance a reporter was interviewing winning race driver Brandon Brown after his victory and while the camera was on, the crowd began their FJB chant. The reporter could not cut away right in the middle of her interview and the chant was clearly being heard, so she tried to cover it up by saying,

"Listen to this crowd chanting for you "let's go Brandon".

Anyone with ears knew that this was not true. And yet this is how desperate the left has become to push and protect the failed agenda of the Democrat Party. It was such a ludicrous attempt at deception that the phrase "Let's go Brandon" has become symbolic of leftist gaslighting.

This also is what the absence of truth looks like.

Maybe this book should have been more appropriately titled American Cruci-Fiction.

AFTERWORD

First they came for the Jews
and I did not speak out
because I was not a Jew.

Then they came for the Communists
and I did not speak out...

Then they came for me
and there was no one left
to speak out for me.

Martin Niemöller

Final Word

This book is dedicated to DB my friend and colleague and his spirit.

All he really wanted to do was just help kids in any way that he could and whatever his flaws he should be recognized for that-something the cancel culture will never do.

Before I sign off I just wanted to make a final appeal to any liberals who happen to read this work. Many of you may not have liked the character of former president Donald Trump but during his time in office not a single one of you leftists were persecuted or punished for your beliefs. Not a single one of you lost a single freedom. Under the current Biden regime those same freedoms and liberties of conservatives are under assault every single day. As many segments of our society have become dominated by the liberal perspective such as the arts, education, government and the media, conservatives have been accustomed to keeping their views private for the sake of remaining employed in such environments. That in itself is wrong but conservatives recognized the reality of it and learned to live with it.

But the cancel culture under the Biden administration has evolved into a whole different entity branding hard working law abiding fellow American conservatives as deplorable, racist, domestic terrorists, white supremacists and insurrectionists as an excuse to silence, de platform, harass, dox intimidate, fire from their jobs, arrest, imprison and dare I say even kill, for the crime of voicing a different opinion then yours.

This is a direct attack on our First Amendment, our Constitution, the bill of Rights and the freedoms of our citizens that those documents entail. This is wrong because it goes against everything that this country was founded on. You KNOW it's wrong. We may not agree with each other but we should be free to express those differences without fear of retribution. As free as you were under Trump because in the end we are all Americans. This can't be the America that you want. It doesn't matter who you voted for, you must stand up with us for the right of all Americans to be free to speak their minds.

I ask you to remember DB. He was one of you. He considered himself part of the regime. He sold his soul for the cause and it turned on him in the blink of an eye and devoured him. I've said many times in this book that cancel culture knows no bounds and that's what separates it from anything else in the past. Today we conservatives are the target but it is only a matter of time before it comes for you. Remember the cancel culture can turn on a dime and already has. There are many liberals such as Joe Rogan, etc. who have been taken down and eaten by the very movement that they thought they were a part of. And finally this piece of history, as was said about the French Revolution and the Reign of Terror that followed-this is a revolution that will eat its own children.

Thank you in advance. Robert Sneider.

WORKS CITED

Burrows, Edwin G. *Forgotten Patriots.* New York: Basic Books, 2008.

Carlson, Tucker. *Ship of Fools.* New York: Free Press, 2018.

Chaffetz, Jason. *The Deep State.* New York: Broadside Books, 2018.

Codevilla, Angelo. The Ruling Class. New York: Beaufort Books, 2010.

Devine, Miranda. *The Laptop from Hell.* New York: Post Hill Press, 2021.

Friedrichs, Rebecca. *Standing Up to Goliath.* New York: Post Hill Press, 2018.

Graber, Mary. *Debunking Howard Zinn.* Washington: Regenery History, 2019.

Hanson, Victor Davis. *The Dying Citizen.* New York: Basic Books, 2021.

Hartman, Andrew. *A War for the Soul of America.* Chicago: The University of Chicago Press, 2015.

Jarrett, Gregg. *The Russia Hoax.* New York: Broadside Books, 2018.

Larsen, Erik. *In the Garden of Beasts.*

Levin, Mark R. *Unfreedom of the Press.* New York: Threshold Editions, 2019.

Malkin, Michelle. *Open Borders Inc. Who's Funding America's Destruction?* Washington DC: Regnery Publishing, 2019

McCourt, Frank. *Teacher Man.* New York: Scribner, 2005.

Meacham, Jon. *The Soul of America.* New York: Random House, 2018.

O'Reilly, Bill. *The United States of Trump.* New York: Henry Holt and Company, 2019.

Orwell, George. *Animal Farm.* Signet.

Orwell, George. *1984.*

Philbrick, Nathaniel. *The Last Stand.* New York: Penguin Group, 2010.

Schweizer, Peter. *Profiles in Corruption.* New York: Harper Collins, 2020.

Shaara, Michael. *The Killer Angels.* New York: Ballantine Books, 1974.

Shenon, Philip. *A Cruel and Shocking Act, The Secret History of the Kennedy Assassination.* New York: Henry Holt and Co., 2013.

Smith, Lee. *The Plot Against the President.* New York: Center Street, 2019.

Watson, Robert P. *The Ghost Ship of Brooklyn.* New York: Da Capo Press, 2017.

White, Theodore. *The Making of the President 1960.* New York: Barnes and Noble Books, 1961.

APPENDIX A

Colonial Trade Game

Rules-Each colony gets 1000 dollars
Each item costs 50$ except ships =100$
Government institutions cost 100$
Each colony must acquire every kind of food item from the other colonies
Each colony must keep at least! of each item that they produce.

NE COLONIES

FURS
LUMBER
FISH
SHIPS

MIDDLE COLONIES

WHEAT

GOVERNMENT

FIRE DEPT SCHOOLS
ROADS JAILS
CHURCHES

RICE
SUGAR
TOBACCO

SOUTHERN COLONIES

COTTON
CORN
FRUIT
VEGETABLES

ENGLAND

POTS,PANS VESSELs
TOOLS
WEAPONS
TEA
GLASS

APPENDIX B

Letter to Principal

It has recently come to my attention that the only information an administration official of a school is permitted to release about one of its teachers to prospective employers is attendance related matters. This is in direct opposition to what you personally stated to me when I informed you of my intent to apply for alternative employment-even when injecting your input was not required by the prospective employer.

Your statement to me was to the effect that you had checked with your legal department and that you felt that it was your responsibility to inform a prospective employer of my performance rating situation at ——————.

Since I had applied to other schools and since we believe this to be incorrect and a violation of my rights, there is an investigation into the matter. If evidence is discovered that you provided employers with negative information on my behalf, and that a hiring decision was impacted, yourself, the city, and the DOE will be implicated in a lawsuit.

APPENDIX C

UFT Hearing for ——

Credentials

My name is Robert Sneider and I have been employed at——— since Sept of ——— after successful completion of the Teach NYC conversion program in special education. Before that I earned a BA in History/Teaching from Merrimack College in North Andover Mass where I attended on a full hockey scholarship. After graduation I played professional hockey in Michigan for the International Hockey League before being employed in the private sector in the electronics industry. I entered the teaching profession after a successful completion of the fellows program Teach NYC. I was appointed under a reciprocal NH regular education ss license. I was recruited to teach science to special education grades 5-8 even though I hadn't taken a science class since high school, and it was not my major.

In this period of time I earned a dual masters in Special education and education with a 3.95 gpa and passed all the state's requirements for sped certification including multi subject special education instruction and have achieved Highly Qualified Status.

I was the first teacher from ———— (even though I was a rookie at the time) to participate in the Globe Science program and the only teacher to be Globe Science certified for the last 5 years running. My participation in that program has resulted in thousands of dollars of equipment being awarded to our school's science department in the form of digital microscope, gps finders and an electronic weather station valued at over 2000 dollars.

I have also been a member of the Telling America's Story social studies program in recent years and have been awarded mentor/historian status for those efforts.

I have participated in professional development at the Museum Of Natural History that has resulted in their mobile museums paying visits to our school for 3 years in a row.

In addition, I have earned certifications in peer mediation and conflict resolution, was selected to be a mentor at————.

Currently I am in the process of writing my dissertation for a PsyD in psychology having completed all the required coursework with a 3.93 gpa.

I was also selected to run the school newspaper, yearbook, participate in afterschool programs and had received various commendations from the school in this period.

I have writings on historical subjects that have been published and are currently available on the internet.

Aside from my student teaching I had never taught before and despite this lack of experience, training, and content knowledge I achieved 4 years of satisfactory performance reviews (3 under the current administration). If you consider that to be an average of 3 formal observations a year and a year-end assessment grade, that equals 16 straight out of 16 assessment opportunities that a satisfactory grade was achieved.

In addition, I was also granted tenure by this principal.

Point Of Reference

In the spring of —— there was an altercation (see incident report) that involved extended day students. The end result of that incident was that Principal——— and I disagreed over the proposed course of action He intended to reprimand me and put a letter in my file. The meeting was attended by ——— who was the UFT representative at the time (see report notes). I indicated to Mr. ———— that if a letter was put in my file that I would grieve the incident and the resulting investigation would reveal that there were more students in my room than was allowed by special education regulations. He decided against placing a letter in my file.

I contend that this is the reference point and the crux of the unsatisfactory performance ratings that were to follow and continue up until the present time.

My Side

Barely a month after the aforementioned incident in ——— Principal ———— attempted to excess me (see grievance report) even though I had seniority over other teachers in the school. This was barely 10 months after he granted me tenure because as he stated I was a valuable addition to the school and a keeper and had assigned Mr.——— a recently retired veteran science teacher to advise me.

His contention now was that I was out of license (which I had been from the beginning) and advised me not to contest it with the reasoning that being an ATR was a "good situation". Of course, I contested it with the UFT (documentation should be on file) and spent the summer with no specific assignment and being listed on the ATR list.

I reported to work in the fall of———and Principal ——— gave me a program the day before school started, apparently realizing that he as unlikely to prevail in an excess hearing. I was given a room and assigned to teach special education social studies, although this was still not my appointed license area.

The room was a disaster (it took two weeks of intense work for myself and a paraprofessional to make it presentable) and I was never given any social studies textbooks. On Sept 11 (only the second week of school) I was observed and given an unsatisfactory review on the basis that my lesson did not follow the textbook material, even though I had no textbooks to work with. Subsequently, (a few months into the school year) some old tattered soft covered texts were discovered in a closet and have been utilized but there is only 7 of these for 29 students, clearly an inadequate supply. (See example)

It was the first unsatisfactory observation I had received in my entire time in the school (and has been followed by a litany of the same) and was the trigger point for justification in subjecting me to a constant pattern of scrutiny, observation, meetings, and lesson plan criticism, all under the facade of offering "assistance".

It is my contention that this was never the intent of this principal and his administration but rather to find any incident of non-compliance that could be written up and placed in my file and when none were available, they were not above construing events to fit their circumstances in portraying me in an unfavorable light. Considering that in the first 4 years of my employment not one letter was placed in my file and the number in the last **12 months alone, is around 2 dozen, one might imply a pattern of excessive harassment.**

If the general assumption of any reasonable person is that a teacher generally improves his professional skills and expertise in the classroom through experience, exposure to models of excellence and continued professional development and content knowledge, one would reasonably have to assume that I am a more accomplished professional now than I was in my first 4 years.

I have now failed every formal and informal observation since the incident of —— (6/6 U ratings after going 16/16 S ratings.) How did I suddenly become an incompetent classroom teacher who in the beginning of my career could do no wrong and now cannot do anything right?

I contend that this illusion is a contrived one that exists only in the eyes of this administration.

It was an impression created and perpetrated by a coerced and compromised administration led by a principal jaundiced by an obsession with retribution for a teacher who stood up for what he thought was morally and professionally right.

In the spring of —— I was offered the opportunity to have my inevitable U rating changed to a satisfactory rating if I agreed to resign from the NYC education system. I declined.

Evidentiary Defense

In addition to my presentation of my own viewpoint with respect to specific occurrences and the refuting of specific allegations, I offer the following evidence in my defense.

Of all the professionals in-house and outside of the school who were in my room for observations or consultation, including Mr. —— and his wife who was a consultant for the DOE, Mr. ——— head of the SS dept, Mr. ——— head of the Sped dept, ———— OSEI consultant and Mr. —— AP of Sped, the ONLY negative references I received regarding my academic presentations were from this principal and his administration(and only after the incident of————)

To this day I have never been provided with a model of instruction from this administration despite repeated requests to this effect.

How is it that my lessons were repeatedly condemned for being unsatisfactory when during the observations the students were engaged, well behaved for the most part and produced the desired results from their efforts, as my paraprofessionals in the room can attest?

How is it that my lesson plans were repeatedly condemned for lack of academic rigor, especially one I submitted about the presidential inauguration and yet that same lesson was incorporated by Ms. —————head of the English Language Arts department and presented to the entire school as an inauguration assignment during the inauguration day proceedings. (See lesson plan)

How is it that my model of the Revolutionary War "trade game" became an example for other teachers in the social studies department to teach the events leading up to the Declaration of Independence and is being proposed for professional development by the head of the social studies department Mr. ———.

How is it that I was the ONLY teacher to have both my lesson plans accepted by the TAH program as models for teachers in all the districts that they represent and is on their current website available to all teachers everywhere? These were lessons that had to be demonstrated in front of peers who had achieved PhD and master's level academic achievement at ——— University. (See website printout)

How is it that in previous years other teachers were sent to my science labs to observe my methods of hands-on instruction? I would cite a previous evaluation from Mr.—— to the effect that –when it comes to hands-on instruction Mr. Sneider may be one of the best in the building.

To this day I have never been supplied with an adequate number of the required social studies textbooks for either of my 7th or 8th grade classes, despite repeated requests for compliance. The response from the administration is that it is not our responsibility. However, if my lesson plans are to be developed and the curriculum adhered to, based on the materials that are provided to the students and that supply is inadequate for instructional purposes, then how can that be the criteria for the purposes of observation and evaluation? It is my contention that if materials on which performance is to be judged cannot be provided, then the criteria itself is rendered invalid.

How is it that through my continued participation in professional development programs such as TAH and Globe Science and being placed in a content area that is my field of expertise that I have become a less accomplished educator than I was in my first year?

If my methods of instruction and adherence to the POEM model were apparently unfailingly delivered in a satisfactory manner during my first four years of teaching, how is it that when the only thing that changes in that equation is the content area—and the content area is now enhanced because it is the field of expertise by way of a bachelor's degree, subsequent certification and continued professional development—how is it possible for that instruction to deteriorate to a level considered unsatisfactory?

This would seem to run contrary to common sense and conventional logic unless one realizes that this has been a contrived and concerted effort to undermine the efforts of a teacher who has always put the education of his students first, has strived for excellence in the classroom as well as trying to improve the learning environment of the school, has always presented himself as a role model and conducted himself in a professional manner.

This continues to the present in which I have been assigned to teach a regular education social studies class. I feel that the only reason I have been given this assignment is because it is an attempt to place me in my licensed area (was the U rating in my special education class of — invalid because it was outside my appointed license) even though I have to go out of my room to teach it and the logistics are proving to be a detriment to adequate instruction at the expense of the students education. I still have no textbooks; I have already been reprimanded in writing for cross teaching subject material and have already received an unsatisfactory formal observation. Also, there is a pattern of cancelled and rescheduled meetings that is disruptive and insidiously unprofessional in its nature and conduct by this administration.

I feel the evidence is justifiable and warrants an overturning of the U rating I received so that I might apply for transfer to another school where my talents might be more appreciated and where my departure is what Mr. ———–—— desires.

APPENDIX D

Excerpt from David McCollough Jr. Commencement Speech

No commencement is life's great ceremonial beginning, with its own attendant and highly appropriate symbolism. Fitting, for example, for this auspicious rite of passage, is where we find ourselves this afternoon, the venue. Normally, I avoid clichés like the plague, wouldn't touch them with a ten-foot pole, but here we are on a literal level playing field. That matters. That says something. And your ceremonial costume... shapeless, uniform, one-size-fits-all. Whether male or female, tall or short, scholar or slacker, spray-tanned prom queen or intergalactic X-Box assassin, each of you is dressed, you'll notice, exactly the same. And your diploma...but for your name, exactly the same.

All of this is as it should be, because none of you is special.

You are not special. You are not exceptional.

Contrary to what your trophy suggests, your glowing seventh grade report card, despite every assurance of a certain corpulent purple dinosaur, that nice Mister Rogers and your batty Aunt Sylvia, no matter how often your maternal caped crusader has swooped in to save you...you're nothing special.

Yes, you've been pampered, cosseted, doted upon, helmeted, bubble wrapped. Yes, capable adults with other things to do have held you, kissed you, fed you, wiped your mouth, wiped your bottom, trained you, taught you, tutored you, coached you, listened to you, counseled you, encouraged you, consoled you and encouraged you again. You've been nudged, cajoled, wheedled and implored. You've been feted and fawned over and called sweetie pie. Yes, you have. And, certainly, we've been to your games, your plays, your recitals, your science fairs. Absolutely, smiles ignite when you walk into a room, and hundreds gasp with delight at your every tweet. Why, maybe you've even had your picture in the Townsman! And now you've conquered high school…and, indisputably, here we all have gathered for you, the pride and joy of this fine community, the first to emerge from that magnificent new building…

But do not get the idea you're anything special. Because you are not.

The empirical evidence is everywhere, numbers even an English teacher can't ignore. Newton, Natick, Nee…I am allowed to say Needham, yes? ...that has to be two thousand high school graduates right there, give or take, and that's just the neighborhoods. Across the country no fewer than 3.2 million seniors are graduating about now from more than 37,000 high schools. That's 37,000 valedictorians… 37,000 class presidents… 92,000 harmonizing altos… 340,000 swaggering jocks… 2,185,967 pairs of Uggs. But why limit ourselves to high school? After all, you're leaving it. So, think about this: even if you're one in a million, on a plant of 6.8 billion that means there are nearly 7,000 people just like you. Imagine standing somewhere over there on Washington Street on Marathon Monday and watching sixty-eight hundred yous go running by. And consider for a moment the bigger picture: your planet, I'll remind you, is not the center of its solar system, your solar system is not the center of its galaxy, your galaxy is not the center universe. In fact, astrophysicists assure us the universe has no center; therefore, you cannot be it. Neither can Donald Trump… which someone should tell him… although that hair is quite a phenomenon.

"But, Dave," you cry, "Walt Whitman tells me I'm my own version of perfection! Epictetus tells me I have the sparks of Zeus." And I don't disagree. So that makes 6.8 billion examples of perfection, 6.8 billion sparks of Zeus. You see, if everyone is special, then no one is. If everyone gets a trophy, trophies become meaningless. In our unspoken but not so subtle Darwin competition with one another – which springs, I think, from our fear of our own insignificance, a subset of our dread of mortality – we have of late, we Americans, to our detriment, come to love accolades more than genuine achievement. We have come to see them as the point – and we're happy to compromise standards, or ignore reality, if we suspect that's the quickest way, or only way, to have something to put on the mantelpiece, something to pose with, crow about, something with which to leverage ourselves into a better spot on the social totem pole. No longer is it how you play the game, no longer is it even whether you win or lose, or learn or grow, or enjoy yourself doing it… Now it's "So what does this get me?" As a consequence, we cheapen worthy endeavors, and building a Guatemalan medical clinic becomes more about the application to Bowdoin than the well-being of Guatemalans. It's an epidemic – and in its way, not even dear old Wellesley High School… where good is no longer good enough, where a B is the new C, and the midlevel curriculum is called Advanced College Placement. And I hope you caught me when I said, "one of the best." I said "one of the best" so we can feel better about ourselves, so we can bask in a little easy distinction, however vague and unverifiable, and count ourselves among the elite, whoever they might be, and enjoy a perceived leg up on the perceived competition. But the phrase defies logic. By definition there can be only one best. You're it or you're not.

If you've learned anything in your years here, I hope it's that education should be for, rather than material advantage, the exhilaration of learning. You've learned, too, I hope, as Sophocles assured us, that wisdom is the chief element of happiness. (Second is ice cream…just an fyi) I also hope you've learned enough to recognize how little you know...how little you know now...at the moment...for today is just the beginning. It's where you go from here that matters.

As you commence, then, and before you scatter to the winds, I urge you to do whatever you do for no reason other than you love it and believe in its importance. Don't bother with work you don't believe in any more than you would a spouse you're not crazy about, lest you too find yourself on the wrong side of a Baltimore Orioles comparison. Resist the easy comforts of complacency, the specious glitter of materialism, the narcotic paralysis of self-satisfaction. Be worthy of your advantages. And read... read all the time... read as a matter of principle, as a matter of self-respect. Read as a nourishing staple of life. Develop and protect a moral sensibility and demonstrate the character to apply it. Dream big. Work hard. Think for yourself. Love everything you love, everyone you love, with all your might. And do so, please, with a sense of urgency, for every tick of the clock subtracts from fewer and fewer; and as surely as there are commencements there are cessations, and you'll be in no condition to enjoy the ceremony attendant to that eventuality no matter how delightful the afternoon.

The fulfilling life, the distinctive life, the relevant life, is an achievement, not something that will fall into your lap because you're a nice person or mommy ordered it from the caterer. You'll note the founding fathers took pains to secure your inalienable right to life, liberty and the pursuit of happiness – quite an active verb, "pursuit" – which leaves, I should think, little time for lying around watching parrots roller-skate on YouTube. The first President Roosevelt, the old rough rider, advocated the strenuous life, Mr. Thoreau wanted to drive life into a corner, to live deep and suck out all the marrow. The poet Mary Oliver tells us to row, row into the swirl and roil. Locally, someone... I forget who...from time to time encourages young scholars to carpe the heck out of the diem. The point is the same: get busy, have at it. Don't wait for inspiration or passion to find you. Get up, get out, explore, find it yourself, and grab hold with both hands. (Now, before you dash off and get your YOLO tattoo, let me point out the illogic of that trendy little expression – because you can and should live not merely once, but every day of your life. Rather than You Only Live Once, it should be You Live Only Once...but because YLOO doesn't have the same ring, we shrug and decide it doesn't matter.)

None of this day-seizing, though, this YLOOing, should be interpreted as license for self-indulgence. Like accolades ought to be, the fulfilled life is a consequence, a gratifying byproduct. It's what happens when you're thinking about more important things. Climb the mountain not to plant your flag, but to embrace the challenge, enjoy the air and behold the view. Climb it so you can see the world, not so the world can see you. Go to Paris to be in Paris, not to cross it off your list and congratulate yourself for being worldly. Exercise free will and creative, independent thought not for the satisfaction they will bring you, but for the good they will do others, the rest of the 6.8 billion – and those who will follow them. And then you too will discover the great and curious truth of human experience is that selflessness is the best thing you can do for yourself. The sweetest joys of life, then, come only with the recognition that you're not special.

Because everyone is.

Printed in the United States
by Baker & Taylor Publisher Services